linea nigra

Also by Jazmina Barrera from Two Lines Press

ON LIGHTHOUSES

linea nigra

an essay on pregnancy and earthquakes

JAZMINA BARRERA

translated from Spanish by
CHRISTINA MacSWEENEY

TWO LINES
PRESS

Originally published as *Linea nigra*
Copyright © 2020 by Jazmina Barrera
c/o Indent Literary Agency
www.indentagency.com

Translation copyright © 2022 by Christina MacSweeney

Two Lines Press
582 Market Street, Suite 700, San Francisco, CA 94104
www.twolinespress.com

ISBN: 978-1-949641-58-5
Ebook ISBN: 978-1-949641-31-8

Cover design by Gabriele Wilson
Cover art copyright © Loie Hollowell, courtesy of Pace Gallery
Design by Jessica Sevey

Printed in the United States of America

Library of Congress Cataloging-in-Publication Data:
Names: Barrera Velázquez, Jazmina, 1988– author. | MacSweeney,
Christina, translator. Title: Linea nigra / Jazmina Barrera;
translated by Christina MacSweeney. Other titles: Linea nigra.
English Description: San Francisco, CA: Two Lines Press,
[2022] | Summary: "Personal essays about pregnancy interwoven
with references to pregnancy in art and literature" --Provided by
publisher. Identifiers: LCCN 2021036586 | ISBN 9781949641301
(hardcover) | ISBN 9781949641318 (ebook). Subjects: LCSH: Barrera
Velázquez, Jazmina, 1988--Translations into English. | Pregnancy. |
Motherhood. | Breastfeeding. | LCGFT: Essays. Classification:
LCC RG551 .B3213 2022 | DDC 618.2--dc23 LC record available at
https://lccn.loc.gov/2021036586

1 3 5 7 9 10 8 6 4 2

This book is supported in part by an award from the
National Endowment for the Arts.

To whom it concerns (Silvestre, Alejandro, and Tere),
and to whomsoever it may concern

contents

I
the pregnant image

This morning, in the waiting room, I came across a calendar of astronomical events. There will be a meteor shower this year, a supermoon in December, a partial lunar eclipse in Asia and, in a few months' time, a partial eclipse of the sun in Mexico.

On the way back home—surprised, excited, disconcerted—I suddenly thought: I'm never going to be alone again. Not really alone. That thought was terrifying and joyful.

―――

Pregnancy is a fruit bowl. The apps tell you which fruit your fetus resembles each week as it grows. But none of the apps are written in Mexico, so they don't take into account the wide variety of fruit we have here, the many different sizes of mangos and avocados. Alejandro says that Mexican mandarins are the same size as Chilean

7

oranges and Chilean mandarins are the size of Mexican limes. Plus, what I simply call a *limón*, he calls a *limón de pica*, and what he calls a *limón*, is for me a yellow lime.

A few days ago we went for an ultrasound and heard the heartbeat. The nurse said it was very strong. The fetus is the size of a blueberry, and a large part of its body is taken up by that strongly beating heart. It's hard not to feel affection for a creature the size of a blueberry with a heart, a creature that is almost nothing except a strongly beating heart.

———

I always used to like the smell of bread; I dreamed up a perfume called *Bakery*, but now the scent that wafts from the bag, even the idea of bread and jam, produces instant, startling bouts of nausea. I tell Alejandro about this and he advises me to write down everything that is happening to me so I won't later forget. I don't tell him that I've already started, since the notion of writing a pregnancy diary feels a little hackneyed. In fact, it's such a cliché that the book *What to Expect When You're Expecting* recommends the practice.

I'm also rereading Maggie Nelson's *The Argonauts*. Today I came to the part where she says that no one talks enough about the darker aspects of pregnancy. She didn't have an easy time of it: she was very frightened and had to face a number of difficult situations.

She felt that she was close to death. The thought that pregnancy could have such harrowing moments had never occurred to me. My mother and the other women around me had only talked about a miraculous transformation, the incredible experience of childbirth, and now it turns out that they had nausea the whole time and felt awful. But they go on saying all that stuff. Of course, there's joy too, heaps of it; like when we talk about names or imagine the child's face. But I saw that coming, I expected it; the darkness was a surprise.

I'm having a hard time believing that almost half the human race has gone through this. It's the most ordinary thing in the world but it seems so different to me, so uncomfortable and unsettling.

The first time my mother's work received critical recognition—I was three or four years old at the time—was for a series of large format abstract paintings on the theme of the color red. But right in the middle of that moment of success, she decided to start a new series, a tribute to the abstract expressionist Ad Reinhardt: a collection of canvases that were impossible to photograph or sell, a treatise on the color black and its limits. Over the years, during visits to galleries and museums, my mother would explain how to look at such paintings as Rothko's black-on-blacks. She patiently taught me the technique for training one's vision to see the black within the black: the opaque blacks, the brilliant blacks, the reddish, purplish, and almost gray blacks. Some years after her black series, during an art class I took as a teenager, I began to understand the expertise needed to distinguish, mix, and balance the various tones of black; the difficulty of painting them as she did, without visible brushwork, making those matte blacks absorbent, the black of emptiness. When I think about what the world is like from the perspective of the uterus, I remember those paintings and the lessons she gave me on seeing in the dark.

—w—

The discussion about girls' names is reaching a stalemate. For a start, names ending in *S* or *Z* are out because the paternal surname is Zambra (nowadays it's possible to use the mother's surname first, but I really don't like mine). I always thought that Paz, peace, was beautiful; but it's not to be. We also ruled out the names of former girlfriends (his exes had lovely names) and boyfriends (very few, and all with more or less horrible names). I was trying out names, almost unconsciously speaking them aloud, when I came to Mar. It sounded gorgeous and Alejandro immediately fell in love with it. It's so original, so simple and beautiful, he said. Why aren't there more people named Mar? What's wrong with naming someone after the sea?

But I instantly regretted that utterance. Mar was my closest teenage friend. Her full name is María del Mar, but we all referred to her as Mar. She's the only Mar I know and I have trouble dissociating the name from the person. It reminds me too much of her, and I want to go on being reminded of her and no one else. Maybe something else. There are hundreds of women's names I like much better. I say them to Alejandro, try to persuade him that Natalia would be good, or Selva, or Josefina, but his mind is set on Mar. Nothing will change it.

—⁓—

I'm back in the land of the living after days when the nausea left me unable to do anything beyond hugging my heated body pillow, or the nearest cushion, or holding Alejandro's hand. I convinced myself that it was like being on a three-month cruise and suffering seasickness (*Mar*-sickness) the whole time. The most intense period of nausea lasts for three months. There were times when I wanted to throw myself overboard; put an end to it all.

Today I had lunch with my friend Uma and for quite some time listened to her talking about the amazing benefits of alternative remedies (acupuncture,

Bach flowers) for the misery she was suffering. As she spoke, I was thinking with veneration of Dramamine. Since starting to take it yesterday I haven't felt nauseous once, and I want to write a thank-you letter to whoever invented it, to say that it has saved my life.

—⁓—

We're still rearranging the apartment. The pregnancy has knocked many of our plans on their heads. Such as: the just-short-of-a-study. We'd bought a desk and chair and placed them in the bedroom adjoining ours. Then we'd had the modem, the alarm, and the telephone moved in there. But now we need a room for the baby. We have to remove all those cables and don't know what to do with the desk; we don't know where we're going to write.

If I'd been aware that I was pregnant, I wouldn't have carried all those boxes when we moved in here. There was a reason why I was so exhausted; running on fumes, as my grandmother used to say.

—⁓—

The internet is full of stories about the difficulties of conceiving a child. A number of my friends have been trying without success for ages. Everything I'd read said that after prolonged use of the contraceptive pill, the body needs about a year to readjust. I stopped taking the pill with that in mind. That year was in the plan, in the order of things. Four weeks later, I was pregnant.

———

Some months ago I applied for a grant that would fund my writing for a year and I've just heard that I've been awarded it. Forget the exclamation marks. I don't know if I'm happy or terrified. With a newborn baby, just when am I going to sit down to write? I can't even remember clearly what the project was.

———

The book calls it "a sense of unreality." My belly is only slightly, only very slightly larger. It's been this size before. If I weren't certain I was pregnant, I wouldn't believe it. I'd think that the nausea and tiredness were something else, and that my late period was due to some hormonal irregularity. I remembered that story by Maupassant, "The Horla." In the early stages, pregnancy is like an invisible being that sucks all your energy and makes you feel ill. When I think about "The Horla" and vampires, I remember this fact: mother's milk is blood passed through a filter. Blood that used to circulate through the veins and arteries and is then converted into milk. When I explain this to other people, it turns out that almost no one is aware of that fact. But it should be widely known, everyone in the world should know it.

———

We decide to put the desk in the dining room and buy another one for the small service room on the roof. I was unwilling to make a final decision about the *where* because I'm afraid of thinking about the *when*: When am I going to be able to write after the birth? At what hour? Of course I'm going to continue writing, I told my mother when she asked if I was prepared to abandon my projects for the next two years. Of course I'm going to continue writing, at least as long as I keep taking the Dramamine.

I've just read "The Third Baby's the Easiest" by Shirley Jackson. A woman is on her way to the hospital to have her third child. Both the drive to the hospital and her labor are protracted, confused, complicated, and painful. The people around her keep insisting that she is "only having a baby," and that the third is "the easiest." My favorite part is when she gets to the hospital and the receptionist asks a series of tedious questions that she has to answer between contractions. When the woman inquires about her job, Jackson replies, "writer." The receptionist says, "I'll just put down housewife." Despite her pain, Jackson repeatedly clarifies that she is a writer and the woman repeatedly says that she's going to put down housewife.

—◊—

I'm reading about the famous Siamese twins Ritta-Christina who lived for only eight months. They shared a vagina and their two legs, but each had her own head. I still haven't felt the apple (a *manzana verde*, according to Alejandro) moving, but I know there's a part of my body that isn't me, that moves of its own accord and has its own genes. A part of me that moves its hands, legs, and mouth, has fingernails and toenails, but nourishes itself on the food I eat, goes where I go, and depends on me for its existence.

I'm sleepy all the time, feel as if I'm anesthetized, as if I'm here without being here. Maybe it's because a portion of me is constructing someone else, or because a portion of me is, at this moment, someone else. Everything is very hazy, but what I want to write is this: pregnancy is a doppelgänger story.

—◊—

The surname *Barrera* is a very heavy burden to bear: a limiting, boring, cacophonous barrier. *Zambra* refers to celebration and noise. It's also the name of a type of boat. A couple of my friends claim they were the first people in Mexico City to give their child its mother's surname, but hers—Prudenco—is evocative, has a lot of character. All children should bear their mothers' surnames, except in the case that the mother's surname means barrier.

On the subject of fiestas, I read about Niki de Saint Phalle, who, in 1966, installed the gigantic figure of a recumbent woman—*Hon* (*She*)—in a Stockholm gallery. Visitors to the installation were able to enter the interior of the brightly colored sculpture through the vagina. Inside, there was an exhibition of fake paintings, a milk bar in the right breast, and a planetarium in the left. Niki called it "a celebration," "the return to the womb."

—ⁿⁿ—

For no particular reason, I've spent a lot of time trying to understand and translate into Spanish a couple of sentences written by Megan O'Rourke: "A mother is beyond any notion of a beginning. That's what makes her a mother: you cannot start the story."

I'm getting those lines mixed up with a poem by Katie Schmid called "The Boatman":

In the afterlife the first face I see is my mother's.
Every mother is the boatman, having once been
    the boat.

I keep trying but the Spanish words won't say what I mean.

—·—

Yesterday I dreamed that I miscarried. I saw the blood and screamed. During my waking hours, I'm not so frightened of miscarrying, because the fetus is still very small: just a few cells. It's too soon to feel excited.

—·—

My mother told me that if I'd been a boy, she'd have called me Silvestre. I grew up hearing that story, and from time to time used to imagine what my life would have been like if I'd been a man and named Silvestre. I found that wild name fascinating, thought that Silvestre would have been braver, less controlling, more cheerful than Jazmina. I suggested the name to Alejandro and he loved it. It's the one we like best so far. (That method doesn't work for girls' names because if Alejandro had been female, he'd have been named Jennifer, which is a name I don't like.)

(Luckily, he's not the kind of man who wants to pass his first name on to his child.)

A girl's name is still a problem. For example, Sara is beautiful, but we've ruled it out because we don't like the rhythm of Sara Zambra. The name came to my mind when a homonymous friend sent me a poem she'd written about her child. In relation to pregnancy, she says it is "The most complete body of work." That phrase returns to me again and again during the day, like an earworm.

—〰—

I thought: everything I do, but principally everything I write during these months, the two of us do and write together. As together as it's possible to be: one in the center of the other.

—〰—

Yesterday I dreamed that I was further along in the pregnancy. Eight months. I was going to have an ultrasound—as is due to happen on Thursday—and on the screen appeared the three-dimensional image of a boy. Suddenly, the boy was an adult and outside of me. His hair was wavy, he was wearing overalls and a red shirt. There was a smile on his face. He didn't look like either of us but he was truly beautiful. I always thought I'd prefer to have a girl, because I'm female, I understand girls. Boys, on the other hand, are a mystery to me. I still think that having a boy must be very difficult, but now I'm excited. I want a boy like the one in my dream.

—〰—

I look for texts on pregnancy as if they were travel guides. Books with advice, books written by psycho-analysts, novels, poems, or essays by pregnant women. It's hard work finding literary sources. A friend told me about Mary Shelley, who was pregnant when she wrote *Frankenstein*. It's obvious but, for all the times I've read the novel, it never occurred to me before: *Frankenstein* is a story about the creation of life, about a man who doesn't so much play at being God as play at being a woman.

The feminist Mary Wollstonecraft died while giving birth to the child who would become Mary Shelley. Mary Shelley, in turn, had four children, al-though only one survived childhood—Clara, whom she was expecting while writing the novel, died just a few days after her birth. It's not unreasonable to suppose that pregnancy was for her, at least in part, a horror story. I think of the passage from *Frankenstein* where the monster comes to life and tries to kill its creator, that terrifying fragment, that postpartum nightmare.

It took Dr. Frankenstein two years to fabricate his monster from pieces of human corpses and ani-mal parts. Two years sounds more reasonable than the meager nine months needed to create a whole hu-man being. Pregnancies should last three, four, five years and be less radical, more gradual. My reasons for thinking this have nothing to do with the evolutionary condition that causes newly born humans to be much more vulnerable than the majority of mammals, who can already walk and practically fend for themselves at birth. I think this because pregnancy seems a titanic, supernatural task, incomprehensible and miraculous. I don't understand how it happens so quickly.

But I'm not kidding myself. I know that it's not me creating the child; it's my blood, my lungs, that craziness of genes. It feels as if someone else were using me to fabricate another human being, someone who isn't me; my hands are outside my womb, I have no idea what's going on in there, and although I read that the fetus already has lungs, eyes, and hair, I'll never be able to explain how it's happening. It all sounds so improbable, like a hallucination or something from a gothic novel.

———

Marlene Dumas painted a canvas called *Pregnant Image*: a portrait of a kneeling woman wearing an unbuttoned blue blouse over her naked body. The large, dark nipples and huge belly give the sense that she is perhaps seven or eight months into her pregnancy. It took Dumas two years to paint the woman, but that isn't obvious because the brushstrokes look decisive, rapid. The woman's face is blue, like the blouse, but the rest of the body is pale. The composition was based on a number of photographs, including some of the artist herself when she was carrying her daughter Helena in 1989, but it's as if the head doesn't belong to the body. That's how I sometimes feel now; as if my head doesn't belong to my body.

Alejandro is worried that the *guagua*—his word for baby—isn't going to like tomatoes or onions because I'm not eating either of them while I'm pregnant. I've never had a very good appetite; there are too many things I don't like and I hate the sensation of being full. But nowadays, I'm hungry as hell, hungrier than I ever was before. I feel so unlike myself. Whole sections of what I used to associate with *me*, with my personal narrative, have changed. "Your body will never be the same again," my gynecologist told me. I don't remember the context, perhaps she was just feeling malicious.

When my mother was pregnant, she had a craving for meat. A lifelong vegetarian, she started eating bacon and hamburgers. On the other hand, what made her feel most nauseous was a song, "La Puerta de Alcalá," which was all the rage then.

In a poem, a love song Sor Juana Inés wrote for the Countess of Paredes, who was then pregnant with her son José, she mentions the countess's craving for nuts.

This is what Sor Juana writes about the dual body of pregnancy:

> when with two souls
> you were, although there was no need
> to be with child
> for you to have a thousand souls;

And then later:

> when, while not a miracle,
> there was found in your beauty
> two bodies in one place,
> two forms but one flesh.

—◦◦◦—

Natalia Ginzburg wrote an essay on abortion, in favor of a woman's right to choose, in which she says that the child in the womb is "a form without voice or eyes…the pale distant sketch of a person…a concrete individuality and a real living possibility." On the decision of whether or not to give life to someone, she says, "If we stop to think about what fate might hold for us, we wonder whether it might not be rational, just, and proper never to choose life and always nothingness." And again: "Loving life and believing in it also means loving pain; it means loving the era in which we are born and the depths of its horror; and it means loving the darkness and tremendous unpredictability of fate."

I've never been so strongly in favor of decriminalizing abortion as now, when I'm pregnant. This brutal transformation of the body should only occur if the woman is willing, if she wants it fervently. Absolutely no woman who doesn't want to go through all this should be obliged to do so.

I think this, and I write it, and then I read the very same thought in *The Argonauts*: "Never in my life have I felt more pro-choice than when I was pregnant."

When I was six, my mother gave me a picture book called *¿Cómo se hacen los niños?* In answer to that question of how babies are made, it explained sexual reproduction through two characters, both of them naked in all the illustrations (I often wondered if they were cold). There are several pages about pregnancy, and the one on childbirth notes: "As the child's head is very big, and the neck of the womb quite narrow, it's very hard for the mother to push the child out. That is the most painful part." The book terrified me. The front cover had a couple between the sheets, the woman on top of the man, both of them in the nude. From that moment I began to think that adults slept that way every night, all night long: as a couple, one on top of the other.

—⁓—

I found a poem by Rosario Castellanos that expresses something similar to what I've frequently thought about pregnancy and solitude:

> His body asked to be born, asked me to let him out,
> give him a place in the world,
> supply the time needed for his story.
>
> I consented. And with the wound in which he was born,
> the hemorrhaging of his detachment
> I also lost the last vestige
> of solitude, of an I looking on from behind a window.
>
> I was left open, offered up
> to visitations, to the wind, to presence.

Parto—from the verb *partir*, to depart—is the Spanish term for childbirth. It had never crossed my mind to imagine childbirth as the moment when someone leaves you: the moment of departure and the moment of partition. The moment of splitting into two.

———

I spoke to my friend Tania, who has two children. It was a relief that she understood when I said that I was still waiting for the magical, miraculous bits because, so far, it was all pretty alien. She told me that the magic was sprinkled over the discomfort, the pain, and the sense of strangeness. In relation to pregnancy, Tania had written that it's like being a goldfish bowl. I must reread that.

I've decided to put the fear of miscarriage aside and believe that the baby really is going to be born. If anything goes wrong, I'll cross that bridge when I come to it. We've started looking at cribs for the just-short-of-a-study.

———

Yesterday a noise woke me with a start in the early hours. My grandmother passed the last years of her life in the house next to ours, and every night a nurse used to come to care for her. Sometimes, when the nurse was asleep, my grandmother would try to get up un-assisted and then fall. When that happened, the nurse would come knocking on our door to ask for help. Since that time, now long after my grandmother's death, loud noises in the night have woken me with the same concern that she's had a fall. Yesterday I didn't think about my grandmother; my fear was nameless and I thought of all the future nights when I would awake with this fear.

Alejandro: "That thing about saying 'we're pregnant,' in the plural. I get the sense of it, but it's dumb. Unfortunately, I'm not pregnant. But you are. You're very pregnant."

We've been told it's a boy. For a few months I'm going to be both a woman and a very small boy.

The truth of that epiphany is that I ran to the kitchen and said to Alejandro: "There's a man inside me!"

Ginzburg once more: "The subterranean accord with that hidden form is unspoken; and the relationship between the mother and that living, undiscovered, hidden form is truly the most closed, the most binding, the darkest relationship in the world; it is the least free of all relationships."

—m—

Pregnancy isn't an illness; all the books and articles emphasize that. But I have to admit that, so far, being pregnant feels very much like being ill. I have strange pains, weird sensations. Being a bit of a hypochondriac doesn't improve things. I'm very conscious of all the differences in my body and associate them with pain.

But Alejandro stopped smoking when he found out that I was pregnant and although he rarely complains, I believe that, on the whole, he's come out of the bargain worse.

—m—

I dream a lot more than I used to. Perhaps because I also sleep ten hours or more every night. I have strange, vivid sorts of dreams. Today I was on the top of a tower of light and to get back to earth I had to change my skin, like a snake.

—m—

During pregnancy you're waiting for the arrival of someone you've never met, someone you've imagined, perhaps seen in images, but who will be completely different in real life. Now, when I look in the mirror, I try to imagine myself as a man. I think that Silvestre is going to take after Alejandro, and that's easy: we have photos of him when he was a boy, and I can visualize our son with black hair, his eyes narrowing when he smiles. But I also want to know what the child's going to inherit from me, what part of me might become (or already is) masculine, and how that will happen.

———

In many pre-Hispanic representations of pregnant women, they are carrying pots in their arms or on their heads. It was believed that tamales should be avoided during pregnancy to prevent the child clinging to the womb—the way tamales stick to the pot—and refusing to come out.

The Mexica people thought that mountains could become pregnant and give birth to nations. Caves were wombs. The pot also represents the womb, the place where grain and water are stored. The bodies of the dead were sometimes kept in large pots or caves so that they would return to their place of origin at the center of the earth.

———

Alejandro and I write in a booklet we bought for the birthing class: a mix of ideas and quotations in my scrawl and his perfect handwriting. I love this booklet, it's like a palimpsest. I hope that Silvestre will read it someday, but perhaps it would be better to let him scribble in it when he's old enough.

We already have a long, long list of new terminology that has to be understood and memorized: psychoprophylaxis, oxytocin, relaxin, colostrum, epidural, trichotomy, lithotomy position, episiotomy, vernix, lanugo, prolactin…

It feels like being back in high school, doing a biology test for my teacher, Claudia Rodón.

—⁓—

During her pregnancy, my mother made many self-portraits. They were mainly exercises in painting her face using different techniques. Your face changes when you're pregnant, she tells me. Even though she produced them on an almost daily basis, she has kept only two of those pictures. They are quite large, around seventy centimeters high. The first, in ink and gouache, is a mesh of black lines and cold colors. The second is painted in reds, using acrylic. In both, her hair is pulled back and she has the attentive expression of someone making a self-portrait.

Erandi comes to visit and brings with her a circular piece of cloth to be used as a cover when breastfeeding. It had never occurred to me that I might need such an item. It looks peculiar, uncomfortable.

Erandi says that, at least in the early stages, being pregnant is like the worst hangover ever. Yes. That's it, exactly.

In the past, I'd never taken much notice of women breastfeeding in public. Now I'm conscious of their body language and the obvious discomfort of certain people around them. Some stare at the mother and child, which is understandable; it's so rare to see a woman breastfeeding in public that the act inspires curiosity. Others do everything possible not to look, which is perhaps even more awkward.

The process of the expulsion of the placenta, the afterbirth, in Spanish is called *alumbrar*, to give light. In Nigeria and Ghana it's believed that the placenta is the baby's twin, a shadow that dies in childbirth. It's ritually buried under a tree.

In the natural history museum in Venice, I saw an ancient reproduction of the placenta. It resembled an extraterrestrial creature, a being with a different form of intelligence than ours. Superior to ours.

―᷿᷿―

I discovered Gustave Courbet's *L'Origine du monde* at the age of fourteen, during a visit to the Musée d'Orsay. I was with my mother and although I can't recall her exact words, I remember that she explained the importance of the painting: it was a groundbreaking work, the first time an artist had dared to portray a woman's pubis and vagina. How appropriate, I think now, that for a while it belonged to Jacques Lacan.

―᷿᷿―

The mother of one of my best friends died of bone cancer when he was three. The cancer, he tells me, was already present during her pregnancy. I often think about that friend sharing his mother's body with a tumor. Life and entropy in gestation at the same moment; in the womb, in the bone, one feeding from the other.

―᷿᷿―

My mother says I was a very feminine little girl. She'd read *The Second Sex* and used to dress me in pants and cut my hair very short. She bought me toy cars and footballs, which I managed to transform into dolls so I could play at being mommy.

—⁓—

It's only now that I can imagine what life was like for my mother when she was pregnant; a secret world that only she knew. How difficult it must be for a man, who will never experience pregnancy, to imagine that state. How difficult it will be for the man in the process of construction inside me to ever understand it.

—⁓—

Archaeologists are uncertain whether the Mexica figure of a woman giving birth, displayed in the Bliss Collection in Washington, DC, is in fact Mexica. Many are convinced that it dates from the nineteenth century. But that makes no difference. If they are right, it doesn't reduce the power of the image: the large, open mouth with a full set of teeth, the flared nostrils, the shoulders drawn back, the empty eye sockets raised toward the sky, the head of the child appearing from the vagina, the marks on the stone like veins and arteries. The woman seems strong, more alive than at any other moment in her life, but her skull is the skull of death.

———

The nausea also has metaphorical aspects. For instance, the other night we went to an indoor barbecue and quite suddenly I felt the need to get out of there quickly. I guess it was a combination of the environment and the smoke. The sensation was very much like nausea: a reflex reaction to an unexpected sense of revulsion. In the past, I'd always put up with unpleasant or uncomfortable situations, pretending everything was fine, but that has changed. The revulsion I feel is stronger now, unbearable, because it seems unfair to the baby, who shouldn't have to tolerate anything unpleasant.

———

I found an article that compares two theories. The first proposes that a pregnant woman is a container holding an independent being. The second says that the baby is part of the body of the pregnant woman, as if it were one more organ. I think both theories are correct. The baby is both things at once, and is constantly changing. In the beginning it's a cell of your own body. You are you: what happens at the very early stages of pregnancy happens to you. Gradually that part of you becomes a different person and you increasingly become a receptacle.

This process, according to Simone de Beauvoir, has both sublime and terrifying consequences: "the fetus is part of her [the mother's] body, and it is a parasite exploiting her; she possesses it, and she is possessed by it; it encapsulates the whole future, and in carrying it, she feels as vast as the world; but this very richness annihilates her, she has the impression of not being anything else."

———

I'm not sure just when my feet disappeared from view. Today, while I was standing in the shower, I realized that I couldn't see my belly button either. In the mirror, I note that it's disappearing. It's less deep, not much more than an asterisk now. Soon it will have vanished completely. It's the only visible sign that I once lived inside my mother, that I fed from her and was part of her. The only sign of that prehistory in which I was an embryo, just like any other vertebrate embryo, and so just like all mammals. That's how the transition from being a daughter to being a mother goes, like a slow erasure.

———

My friend Laura is just four weeks further into her pregnancy than me. On the basis of that minimal difference in terms of experience, and because she's fun and lovely, I've decided she's going to be my Virgil. I urgently need a Virgil. She gives me advice about everything: the doctor, the hospital, clothes.

Over the phone, I complain to her about how ill I feel. I give pregnancy a bad name because I'm always going on about the strangeness and the inconveniences and not, for example, how exciting it is to feel him moving inside me. His kicks, his displacements, seem to me like a sort of Morse code: our first communication, deliciously ambiguous and one-way.

My mother reminds me that I shouldn't view the eclipse. A Maya myth from pre-Hispanic times says that the sun is consumed during an eclipse, and if a pregnant woman sees it, her child might be born deformed. In order to neutralize this threat, women used to place an obsidian knife close to their breasts. Even now, when there's an eclipse in Mexico, women carry scissors or sometimes a piece of red string. I don't believe in any of that, but I do have a personal superstition about ignoring my mother's advice. Historically, that has definitely brought me bad luck.

I keep speaking in the plural. If I'm asked how I am, I reply, "We're fine." The baby is moving around like a caged animal. His movements are clearly visible beneath my skin. The sensation of having *something* in my belly is less frequent now than feeling *someone* is in there.

It's said that during the first hour after birth, the baby establishes a new relationship with gravity as the nerve that deals with balance sends out an unprecedented torrent of electrical impulses. The baby inside me is now experiencing what I would if I were floating in outer space.

I think of that great final scene from *2001: A Space Odyssey*, where the old man becomes a Star Child, the fetus observing the earth from some place in the universe.

The uterus is an inner exterior space, a contained universe.

On the second floor of the hospital there's a phantom piano. The kind that plays without a pianist. The music ranges from Bach to The Police without any attempt at continuity between the pieces and, as it's on a mezzanine, it can be heard on all the floors, even in our new gynecologist's waiting room. I think I recognize a song my grandmother used to play on the piano and I go out to hear it more clearly, but it isn't the same tune and I return to the waiting room and sit down next to Alejandro on an upholstered bench. In an aquarium in one corner of the room, a couple of Siamese fighting fish swim around and around with their fins trailing beneath them. We've come to this doctor on Laura's recommendation. A friend of hers used him, and Laura's been seeing him since she got pregnant. On the internet, he's said to be one of the pioneers of the humanization of childbirth, respectful childbirth as opposed to the violence of obstetricians who separate mothers from children, discourage breastfeeding, and mainly carry out C-sections.

Two other pregnant women are in the waiting room and we smile at each other in gravid solidarity. I try to guess how many months they are: six on my right—she still seems to have some energy and is less hunched over; eight or even nine on my left—her belly is definitely weighing her down. I attempt to get a first impression of the doctor from the decor: less pink than the last gynecologist's waiting room, more colorful. Fewer images of women breastfeeding and more abstract forms (there are Miró and Kandinsky prints on the walls). Nevertheless, the coffee table in the center of the room holds the same leaflets advertising stem cell preservation (if my internet searches are right, this is a hugely expensive scam) and infertility treatments. We're soon in the doctor's office. I immediately feel reassured for the dumbest of reasons: the room is full of plants. I assume that they are the result of a certain zest for life, a caring person with a fine botanical understanding. Naturally, all those qualities could belong to the cleaner, but I decide to attribute them to the doctor. He also has photos: a dozen or so images of himself with two little girls, who we think must be his daughters. The smiles of the blond children don't reveal whether they experienced natural childbirth or were the result of C-sections. There's absolutely no sign of the mother. On the table is a dish of candy and a pile of books about humanized childbirth.

The doctor comes in and sits at his computer. He speaks quietly and little, but gives us all the essentials: that he's not one of those clinicians who is going to schedule me for a caesarean so he has more free time and can charge a higher fee, that he supports humanized childbirth, which is to say intervening as little as possible, only when absolutely necessary, using hot water baths for the pain and Maya chairs or any position that allows gravity to assist the birthing process. When he's finished, he leaves a pause for questions. I like that too. I prefer it to the rush my previous doctor

38

always seemed to be in. He confirms that the birth will take place in that hospital and I can bring along a doula if I want. He'll see me once every four weeks until the last two months, when the appointments will be weekly. We feel calm when we leave, happy to have found a sensible doctor.

—⁓—

They say that his sense of taste will never be as keen as it is during these weeks. The taste of the mango I'm eating passes into the amniotic fluid, and he can sense it more strongly than I can.

—⁓—

We're at the birthing class, in a session on the post-natal stage. We're sitting in a circle on chairs that are very uncomfortable, particularly for those, like me, who have already put on 10 kilos. Alejandro is making notes in the booklet in which we intended to write down the most important information we learn in the classes, but in which we in fact note the funny things the teachers and other students say.

One teacher asks if any of us know how long the postnatal period is, and I raise my hand and say your whole life. I expect the other couples to laugh, but they don't, and neither does the teacher. With a very grave expression, she responds, "That's right. Your whole life." Suddenly it doesn't seem all that funny to me either.

Among Alejandro's notes I find these particularly good comments that we heard during the course:

"You have to distract the uterus."
"The assistants love doing the two-finger check."
"It's important to train the perineum."
"I'm one of life's spectators."

Rachel Cusk says that these courses are like taking classes in dying.

—⁓—

We've been given so many baby clothes that they no longer fit in the drawers. I have no idea why I enjoy unfolding and folding them so much. The aesthetic is ridiculous because the baby isn't going to see any of this. At first he will scarcely be able to distinguish colors. It's all for the adults, so that they remember their infancy or attribute who knows what to the baby. Innocence? Warmth?

I'm in my mother's house, drinking tea and talking about a cousin's son. My mother suddenly recalls the first months of my life, the way I used to stare at the window so peacefully. She says she likes observing babies because they still have something of not being, of the nothingness before existence, the other world before and after life.

—⁓—

The day before I was born there was snow and my mother and father drove to the Iztaccíhuatl volcano to see it. My mother thought that there must have been a mix-up with the due date; she felt far too well for someone who was supposed to give birth the following day. The contractions began the next morning. She spent the day resting at my grandmother's. Gran was feeling dizzy, as sometimes happened when she was driving or very nervous. The doctor was out of town, he'd gone to assist in the birth of a doe belonging to the Huichol people. There was a power outage in the small clinic in San Jerónimo. My grandmother was shocked by the lack of resources, by the doctor's casual air. The midwife said that I must be a girl because I was cooperating. My mother pushed three times and I was out.

—⁓—

In a book by Pascal Quignard, I read that fetuses dream while they are in the womb. What can they dream of? Sounds, sensations, tastes?

Alejandro is sleeping and, as he hasn't been feeling too well, I don't want to wake him. It's supposed to be dangerous to look directly at the sun during an eclipse, so I cut a hole in a piece of cardstock to view the reflected image, even though I'm not certain it will work. I put the scissors I made the hole with in the pocket of my shirt and slip silently out into the street. The eclipse must already be underway, but I can't see it because clouds are obscuring the sun. Small clouds, moving quickly. At any moment a patch of sky might clear between them, even if only for a second, and the eclipse will be visible. The piece of card is of no use whatsoever, but there's a puddle on the sidewalk, left over from yesterday's rain, and it's reflecting the cloud covering the sun. I stand near it. The clouds clump together, it looks like a space is going to appear but then it immediately closes up. I'm about to give up when I see the eclipse reflected in the puddle for an instant. The sun looks very small, like a candy with a bite taken out of it. I think that I see him like that too—indirectly, in black and white, distant—through the ultrasound equipment, like the reflection of an astronomical event.

Three months to go before he's born and two years to the next eclipse.

I was thinking of writing an essay about pregnancy. I'm always thinking about writing essays; that is to say, experiments without any commitment to a particular subject, without a climax, a plot, or a predetermined length. I read a few pages from this file to some friends and one of them said, "It's a short story." Pregnancy is transformation in time, it's a retrospective account and—whether you like it or not—there's a plot, a story.

Rosario Castellanos's *The Book of Lamentations* describes how a young woman, Marcela, gives birth during an eclipse. She says that the sun and the moon are battling in the sky, while Marcela's people, the Tzotzil, cry out, play drums, and ring bells to accompany the spectacle. Marcela is wearing a mask made of tree bark to defend her from the eyes of the Demon Pukuj, who is on the loose. She doesn't give details about the Pukuj but it sounds terrifying. Marcela is like a foal that refuses to cross a fast-flowing river. She stands, clutching the strongest column in the house, and the child is born. The umbilical cord is cut on an ear of maize, to ensure that the seeds will be fertile. Marcela is given agua de chile to aid her recovery and when the eclipse is over her mask is removed.

The next day, Marcela goes to the temazcal, a sweat lodge, and through the steam rising from the stones she meets, or rather recognizes, her son.

—〰—

We were watching my belly rise and fall with the baby's kicks when suddenly everything else began to move. Certain that it was an earthquake and not just a truck going past, we rushed to the door. I grabbed the keys from Alejandro because it takes him longer to deal with all the locks, and then I ran. Afterward I thought that I should have waited for him, but when you're pregnant, behaving selfishly feels the same as behaving unselfishly. Looking out for myself is looking out for someone else.

—〰—

There's a scientific study that claims babies enjoy it when their pregnant mothers stroke their bellies. They feel some form of pleasure. Putting your hands on your belly and stroking it when the baby is kicking strongly is an instinctive reaction. Or perhaps it's a form of protection, or just because. I also read that the Babushka dolls I loved so deeply as a child always have two hands on their bellies as a signal that they are pregnant.

Yesterday, at the birthing class, we were told that female mammals usually go into labor at night because there are fewer predators around at that time. The pupils dilate during childbirth, so it's better to have the lights dimmed. In Mexico, during a home birth, it's customary to close the doors and windows so evil spirits can't get in. The house is kept in darkness. The process of bringing a child into the world is called *dar a luz* in Spanish, giving to light, but there's more of night than day about it all. Even when the birth happens during daylight hours, it's like a sort of eclipse: darkness in the day.

A dark line has been gradually appearing on my abdomen. It's called the linea nigra. Apparently, as babies see in high contrast, it enables them to move up the stomach and find the nipples. My body is being covered in signs for someone else, signs that have to be explained to me since I don't know how to decipher them.

I suddenly understand why many men have feared women throughout the ages, considering them to be witches. Beyond any biological explanation (particularly when there isn't one), all those animal instincts, those signs of genes, seem very much like magic.

Alejandro is standing in his pajamas playing with a cup-and-ball (I call it a *balero*, he calls it an *emboque*). I watch him from the couch in the living room. He says that he'll take a shower as soon as he gets the ball in the cup. He doesn't succeed the first time, or the second. On the third attempt he manages it and the floor begins to move. The curtains swing, the plants sway. "Quake," I say. Alejandro tries to unlock the door, but, once again, he's finding it difficult. Again I grab the keys from him. In the street, on the narrow sidewalk by the underpass, we wait for the tremors to stop, but they don't. They feel strong, but we can't imagine, have no way of knowing the magnitude of the earthquake. A little later, we see the photographs and watch news bulletins showing the collapsed buildings with people still trapped inside. We're beginning to understand just how serious it is.

Half the city is practically in ruins. There are still many people under the rubble. In the birthing class, the women cry. They feel guilty for being afraid or sad. Repressing emotions is a crazy form of torture. People ask me if the baby is all right. Of course he's all right, maybe just a little shaken.

I discover that fetuses rehearse crying in the uterus. They cry silently, grimacing and opening their mouths. I can't get the image out of my head: mute screams, like Munch's painting. The womb is supposed to be a sort of primeval paradise: a place where there's no hunger, pain, or cold.

———

In an article entitled "The Grand Shattering," Sarah Manguso writes, "But motherhood is a different sort of damage. It is a shattering, a disintegration of the self, after which the original form is quite gone." For her, motherhood is an earthquake.

———

After many years of struggling to sell her paintings, my mother found an entrepreneur, half-Argentinian, half-Swiss, who became her patron. I saw him only a few times, but remember him as graying, corpulent, and—from the anecdotes my mother tells—I imagine he was a cheerful man with a keen sense of humor. For almost fifteen years, she handed over every single one of her paintings to him. That was three or four a year because, as a perfectionist, she'd spend months and months (and more months) working on the same piece before deciding it was finished. My mother adored her collector. The paintings went straight into his vault, no one else saw them, but that didn't worry her. Painting became a way of carrying on a dialogue with him. As happened in the Renaissance, she began to work with him in mind, for him. Painting as a form of saying thank you, showing her genuine, profound gratitude.

When the collector died a few years ago, his children inherited a total of thirty-five works. The paintings were put into storage on the sixth floor of a building in Colonia Narvarte. The day after the earthquake my mother received a phone call: the building had collapsed. The paintings were buried under the rubble.

It was perhaps during the sixth of my grandmother's seven years with dementia. She could scarcely walk by then, and developed bedsores from lying in the same position for so long. It was midday. My grandmother was sleeping. My mother and I were on the patio. The ground began to tremble and in a flash my mother ran upstairs and returned with Grandma in her arms, as if she were a newborn baby. My grandmother had been tall, but by then she'd shrunk quite a lot and probably weighed less than her daughter. The three of us sheltered under a fig tree in the garden until the tremors passed.

II
linea nigra

In 1787, Élisabeth Louise Vigée Le Brun painted a famous portrait that now hangs in Versailles: *Marie Antoinette and Her Children*. The queen, dressed in red and wearing a powdered wig, is holding a baby as her eldest daughter stands on her right, clutching her elbow. On her other side, a small boy is pointing to the empty cradle that should have contained the youngest of her offspring, who died during the birth.

Vigée Le Brun was a self-taught, hardworking artist who understood public relations. She not only portrayed Marie Antoinette but was also her close friend. Her contemporary males made it their task to establish fierce competition between Vigée Le Brun and another of the few female painters of her time who managed to gain recognition: Adélaïde Labille-Guiard.

One of Labille-Guiard's best-known portraits is *Madame Mitoire and Her Children*. Here, a woman has her head turned toward her eldest son, who looks into her eyes, one arm resting on her shoulder; a baby is latched to the woman's left breast. She's wearing a floral headdress.

In Vigée Le Brun's diaries, the artist says that when she went into labor with her daughter she continued painting between contractions.

Laura tells me about a couple she knows whose house was demolished in the earthquake. They escaped harm because the whole family was at the hospital waiting for the woman to give birth.

I must have been about nine when I watched one of my mother's friends read her palm. Her lifeline was very short, the woman said. She would die young. When I heard that, I ran to the bathroom in tears. My mother tried to console me, saying that if what her friend had said were true, then all soldiers of the same age who died during a war would have lifelines of exactly the same length, which wasn't the case. I wasn't convinced. I hated that friend after that. I still hate her.

On the corner of Etiopía and Vértiz, my mother is working with the military and residents to rescue what remains of her paintings from the ruins. They have already found quite a few, some in better condition than others, some cracked in two. They are also removing belongings: the clothing, jewelry, toys, and furniture of the people who lived in the building. There's a chatroom where they upload photos of all of it in order to find the owners, and on that site my mother found three birthday presents she'd given her patron: Huichol craftwork covered in Czech beads, very fragile but unharmed.

There are still people trapped under the rubble. Apparently some of them weren't killed because they were sheltering under the wooden boards of the paintings. Meanwhile, Alejandro is volunteering in a distribution center a few blocks from home. I feel completely useless, perched below my belly. I help by making phone calls to organize volunteers and watch news bulletins of children being rescued from beneath what was left of their school. Tonight, I suddenly burst into tears and now can't stop crying; when Alejandro hugs me and asks what's wrong, I don't have the words to tell him. Then he says he's sorry. Asking what's wrong is the dumbest thing imaginable. "I'm such a clod," he adds, "that I see you crying and ask what's wrong."

Since becoming pregnant I've been waking every night at around 3 a.m. feeling hungry. Alejandro says that I'm like a sleepwalker. I get up, pour myself a glass of almond milk, and sit in the living room to drink it without turning on the lights. I listen to the sporadic sounds of passing cars, think about what I'd been dreaming, look at the shadows of the plants on the curtains. Alejandro has memorized the names of all the plants so he can introduce the baby to them when he's born. I think about the baby, his white bones made of almond milk. Tonight, sleeplessness is a bore, but I guess I'm going to miss these nocturnal stirrings when he's out.

———

However often I listen to explanations of the workings of the art market, there's a part of me that's never going to understand why it is that if she wanted to buy one of her own paintings, my mother wouldn't be able to afford it.

———

In an album with a pink cover, there's a black-and-white photo of my mother when she was pregnant. My father took it. She's smiling and looking toward the place from where the light is entering. A window, perhaps. Her curly hair falls loose over her shoulders. She's completely naked, lying on one side on a bed with an eight-month pregnant belly. She tells me that she used to spend a lot of time sitting in the sun when she was pregnant, that's why she looks so bronzed.

—⁓—

Whenever Marie Darrieussecq is asked for an author photograph, she sends one of her pregnant and in the nude. The response is almost always a request for a "normal" photo.

—⁓—

My grandmother was a nurse, and a doula before that term was used to indicate women who accompany mothers during childbirth. I know very little about that stage of her life. If only she were still alive to help me not be afraid!

I'm not sure who told me, but apparently when I was born, the first person to hold me was my grandmother, and the first thing she said was, "Here you are."

—⁓—

During one of those sleepless nights, the thought crosses my mind that pregnancy happens *to* you, like dreams.

―――

After two dreadful experiences giving birth to her first children, news of the Lamaze technique, which had originated in France and Russia, came to the ears of my grandmother (and innumerable other women in the sixties). She was captivated by the book *Painless Childbirth: Psychoprophylactic Method* and decided to train to give classes and accompany women during birth. For many years those classes took place in the living room of her home; my mother and her sisters were not allowed to enter but they used to spy through the keyhole. They watched my grandmother explaining how the women should relax and breathe. She hid the book in the underwear drawer of her closet so the children wouldn't see it. But when she left the house, the girls used to take the book from the drawer. They can still describe the anatomical diagrams and the bloody images of women in childbirth.

―――

Laura tells me that fucking when she knew she could get pregnant, with that adrenaline rush, was the best sex she's ever had. I think that was true for me too.

I'm only just beginning to become aware of another thing that happens during pregnancy; the flow of blood to the vulva increases, and with it comes increased sensitivity, so the sensations become more intense and orgasm occurs more quickly. Much more quickly. Sometimes while we're sleeping.

In a beautiful graphic novel, Paloma Valdivia tells the tale of her pregnancy and says of herself and her pregnant friends: "It was our moment for swelling the world. We were making people."

I'd make a great father. That's what I think when people ask me if we want to have more children. I'd love to have another child, if only Alejandro could do the pregnancy part. Now that I know the time, effort, and energy involved, I feel that life and my body will only allow me to be a mother once. But, if it were possible, I know I'd really enjoy accompanying a pregnant Alejandro. I'd support and care for him, hold his hand throughout the ultrasounds. I'd buy him candy, plump his pillows, and help him put on his shoes when he can no longer reach that far down. I know some men envy pregnant women, but I envy those men's power to be part of it all without actually having to go through the experience, to be bystanders and witnesses without becoming mutants.

———

Everything in the photo is askew: the mirror leans to the right, the camera is tilted to the left, as is Diane's head. Her naked body and the camera are reflected in the mirror, but her gaze is outside the mirror; focused somewhere else. She isn't smiling. Her hand is positioned below her breasts, resting on her belly with its slightly prominent navel. She's in her fifth or sixth month. *Self-Portrait, Pregnant, N.Y.C.* is one of a series of photographs that Diane Arbus took in the nineteen-forties to document her pregnancy for her husband, who was fighting in World War II. It was her first child and she was twenty-two years old.

———

I've always had a horror of the Monument to the Mother, that soulless plaza in Colonia San Rafael with gray sculptures: an unbearable notary, a woman holding an ear of maize, and an enormous, obnoxious mother cradling a baby with the face of a tyrant. That art deco sculpture, installed in 1949, was destroyed in the earthquake.

―⁓―

When I was young, my mother's childbirth photos were in one of the family albums, but lying loose because they were contact sheets, and so too large for the pockets. Two black-and-white sheets, each frame so small that you had to hold the paper up close to see the image. At that age, the face masks and surgical caps, my mother's pain-filled face, the image of the bloody crown of my head, were all terrifyingly repulsive.

This afternoon, I ask my mother to bring the contacts along so we can look at them together. They are faded and some are moldy, but you can still make out the scenes. The size and number of photographs makes it possible to reconstruct the narrative, which would be more or less this:

My mother is lying on a couch in the clinic. Behind the couch is a tall jug and piles of books. Beside her, sitting on the floor, is my father, dressed in white, and the midwife, wearing a checked blouse, with her hair in a French braid. The midwife says something to my mother. On another of the clinic's couches sit my grandmother and aunt, first chatting together, then my aunt is reading something and Grandma is stretched out beside her, a blanket draped over her body. Behind the couch, my uncle is massaging my mother's temples; she has her eyes closed. The next image is my mother in a hospital bed with her legs open. My grandmother, father, and aunt stand around her, wearing surgical gowns, caps, and face masks. Then comes my mother's mouth open in a cry of pain and Grandma's nervous face as the doctor's hands take hold of my head. When I'm completely out and they see that I'm female, my father, who wanted a girl, smiles at the camera and makes a victory sign. His mouth is covered by a mask but his eyes are smiling. Then I appear, wet, crying, wrapped in a towel as the doctor listens to my heartbeat through a stethoscope. They bring me to my mother's breast and she smiles. Next, four hands (we can't see any faces) are bathing me in a bowl. Grandma takes charge and dresses me while my mother rests. The last photos are less clear, but we're both dressed and I think we're in Grandma's house. My mother is holding me to her breast; I'm wrapped in a blanket.

The doula told me that women who are the product of natural childbirth are more likely to give birth naturally themselves. I'm not certain if she's referring to a genetic process or the transmission of some form of body knowledge.

~~~

The time is coming for me to start writing the project outline for the grant, before I give birth, while I still have an active brain. I feel like Mario Levrero in

The Luminous Novel but instead of putting things off by playing Minesweeper, I make lists and more lists of things still to be bought for Silvestre's room: a mosquito net, a cover for the changing table, shampoo, and an interminable etc. I have no way of knowing which of all these things is absolutely necessary. I'm like a consumerist squirrel facing the end of the world. I want to ask my grant advisors if I can change my project. I want to write this book: it's the only one I can write for the time being.

———

Frida Kahlo imagined and painted her own birth: a bed with white sheets, and on it a woman, her legs wide open. The birth is almost over: Frida's head is visible, but the rest of her body has yet to come. The baby Frida has the face of an adult, with her characteristic single eyebrow over closed eyes. Her head rests in a pool of blood, alluding to the miscarriage the artist suffered just before starting the painting. The mother's torso and face are covered by a sheet because she died a short time before. Above the bed is a weeping portrait of the Virgin of Sorrows.

———

Before Alejandro and I got married, we lived in an apartment that a friend rented to us for peanuts in

"Strollerland," as the Brooklyn neighborhood of Carroll Gardens is unofficially known. It's a quiet, leafy, residential district and so favored by New Yorkers with very young families. When they decide to have children, they move to this neighborhood full of pharmacies and stores selling baby clothes and toys. Then, when the infants grow up a little, they relocate to places even farther from the city, where the schools were better. Nannies and mothers stroll along the streets of Strollerland with babies of every color and size.

For the greater part of my life I never thought about having children. It's not that I didn't want them, but even the idea of the idea felt stupid to me. The emotional and material conditions I believed necessary seemed like impossibilities. My friends went through "baby fever" phases in which they were crazy to get pregnant, even when they knew that the circumstances of their lives were in no way perfect; I, on the other hand, didn't give the matter a second thought. But I did spend many hours working out how to get ahold of a hypoallergenic cat.

I began to think about having children because I fell in love with Alejandro, and because we were living in Strollerland, surrounded by babies.

—

My cousin was supposed to photograph Laura and I with our swollen bellies in my mother's garden, but he's gotten held up and can't come. So my mother takes out her phone and snaps us sitting on a palm frond mat. She gives us a couple of sarongs to wear halter style that leave our stomachs bare. We're doubled up with laughter because it's such an effort to sit down and stand up.

—•—

I forgot about the feeding shawl Erandi had offered me until the baby shower. I was given another two, and a girlfriend who had a six-month-old baby presented me with a nursing apron. "I never used it, but it might come in handy," she said.

What is it with all these shawls and aprons? What's the message? That breastfeeding in public is indecent, polemical, risky? Apparently it's not obvious that the primary function of breasts is to feed babies; that hungry children can't wait; that women shouldn't have to hide what they are doing. I think all that, but then it occurs to me that the shawls aren't so bad, and might protect me from the unsettling stares of strangers or people I don't trust. They could be a sort of lucky charm to ward off the evil eye.

—•—

It's been years since I've seen my mother give up on a painting, but when I was a child it used to happen all the time. After weeks or sometimes months of work, I'd come home from school one day and the canvas would be blank again. Why didn't she just put it aside and begin a new one? Why did she have to erase the image? What if she changed her mind? I hated when she did that.

—

Mozart's No. 40 was playing as I was born. The doctor asked my mother if he could put it on and she didn't care one way or the other. I'm sure that in such circumstances, you wouldn't give a damn if the music is by Rammstein or Bach, but even so we've been working for hours on an endless playlist for the birth (for first-time mothers, labor can last over twelve hours). These are the criteria: cheerful songs, but not too cheerful. Nothing by LCD Soundsystem or Shakira, no cumbia. Songs about children, about births (some of the former exist, but we still haven't found any examples of the latter). Songs we'd like to be born to. As a consequence of all those limitations, a few fairly ridiculous things slipped in, such as Chava Flores's hilarious "Sábado Distrito Federal." About eighty percent of the playlist is David Bowie.

—◦◦◦—

A pregnant woman, says Sylvia Plath, has nine months "of becoming something other than herself, of separating from this otherness, of feeding it and being a source of milk and honey to it." Plath described her experience of giving birth in detail in her journal, and she also wrote a verse play for radio called *Three Women*, in which the women in question speak from a maternity ward. Two of them lose their babies, and the only one to take her child home says: "There is no miracle more cruel than this."

—◦◦◦—

Another scientific controversy. No one can tell for certain if it's the baby or the woman's body that decides when to initiate labor. Some articles claim that pressure exerted by the baby sets off the chain of hormones that starts the birth process. Our doctor, on the other hand, says it must be the woman's body; otherwise, he tells us, there would be no premature babies, no babies born before they were ready.

The discomfort is becoming unbearable, particularly at night, even though I sleep with a pillow like a giant worm: an enormous letter *C* that supports my back or my belly as the case demands. Alejandro hates it and so do I, but deep down I love it because without it my whole body aches. I bought the worm-pillow when Alejandro was away and he says it's a substitute for him. I'm always in a lousy mood, the days seem to go on forever; I'm worn out and yet restless. If it's the woman's body that decides when labor starts, how is it that I can do nothing to hurry it along?

—

Alejandro isn't keen on the doctor. He hardly ever does ultrasounds and charges a fortune just for measuring my belly. Then he asks if everything is going well and says he'll see us next month. But Alejandro's main reason for hating him is the tone of his voice, because he's a "low talker," to quote from *Seinfeld*. "He starts out speaking at a reasonable volume," Alejandro complains, "but then his voice drops and it's impossible to hear whatever else he says. And of course since we've already started nodding our heads, we keep on nodding and then it would seem crazy to ask him to repeat himself. But when we get home, it turns out that neither of us understood a word of it." But the doctor's imperturbability calms me. He responds to my concerns without the least sign of alarm, and almost always with the same words: "That's normal." The weirdest things are normal in pregnancy, exceptions are the rule. The internet feeds my paranoia, whereas the doctor's slow, almost inaudible voice calms me. "The peace of boredom," Alejandro calls it. I'm due in just a few weeks. Everything is ready: the doctor, the hospital, the crib.

This time the doctor invites us into his office after the checkup and says he has something to tell us. My hands begin to sweat, I imagine a thousand illnesses, defects, problems that might entail a C-section. It's an enormous relief when he gives us the news: he's leaving the hospital. Apparently he's having problems with the administration, and next week he's moving somewhere else, but isn't sure where yet. Alejandro asks, twice, politely but very directly, why he's leaving. The doctor skirts the subject.

Just when I've gotten used to my initial lack of concern, I realize how awkward the situation is. The birth will have to take place in another hospital. We've already visited the maternity unit here and like its large rooms, each with a bathtub and a window looking out onto a leafy courtyard. And the phantom piano, of course. He offers us a couple of other options: an expensive place a long way from our home, or another that is rumored to have suffered earthquake damage. He tells us to visit them and let him know which we prefer.

—ⱳⱳ—

I miss:
    Sleeping on my back
    Eating seafood
    Breathing freely

I'm going to miss:
    His kicks
    The excitement of imagining him

—⁓—

I've reached the limits of my "baby brain," or at least I hope so. That's the term for the forgetfulness, poor concentration, and absentmindedness many women experience with pregnancy, because, it seems, the brain changes; the gray matter and the area of the brain responsible for memory shrink. When a friend came to visit, I wanted to make her tea but mistook the electric kettle (shaped like a teapot) for a normal teapot (we don't have one) and put it on the stove. By the time I realized what I'd done everything had melted and the stovetop was covered in a stinking, black liquid. I think I should stop driving.

—⁓—

As far as is known, the first contemporary self-portrait of a pregnant woman was made by Paula Modersohn-Becker at the beginning of the twentieth century. She painted it just before dying from a pulmonary embolism that occurred during childbirth. She was thirty-one. There's another self-portrait, painted a little earlier, in which she appears to be pregnant, nude from the waist up, with a braid of hair wound around her head, a long string of amber beads around her neck, and her hands resting on her swollen belly; but in this portrait her condition is imagined: she wasn't in fact pregnant. The self-portrait she actually painted during her pregnancy, along with another seventy of her works, was decommissioned, as it was considered to be "degenerate art" and later vanished during an air raid. Nude women, women breastfeeding, self-portraits by a woman as no one had ever before painted one.

—

I pack my hospital bag. Clothing for the newborn. Nursing blouse. Diapers. Blanket. Change of clothes for me. Toothbrush.

The documentary *The Motherhood Archives* shows many women in the fifties doing exactly the same thing. Packing, says the film, to travel to "an unimaginably foreign country."

—

In 2001 my mother spent a few months as an artist-in-residence in New York. I stayed with my grandparents but visited her during the summer. We lived in an apartment in Brooklyn, near the L line. My mother had a studio in Midtown Manhattan, on 58th Street, where she was painting small, round works in pale colors, which looked like the moons of strange planets. I returned to Mexico a few weeks before the planes crashed into the Twin Towers. I was in class on September 11 when the teacher turned on the TV and we watched replays of the images of smoke and chaos. I told the concerned people who asked about her that there was no way my mother had been there because she always refused to go to the World Trade Center. She used to say that it had very bad feng shui: the towers, near the lower tip of the island of Manhattan, where two rivers meet, cut across the phoenix, and according to feng shui, that's awful.

A few hours later, she sent an email. Apparently she was in her studio when the second tower fell and rushed through Manhattan trying to find a place of refuge or some way to get back to Brooklyn. No one had any idea what was going on. In her building, the neighbors were giving her suspicious looks because she didn't hang a flag in her window. The airports were a mess and there was no clear idea of how long it would take her to get back to Mexico. She managed to get out three weeks later, leaving her paintings in the care of the Mexican consulate. She repeatedly asked for the package to be mailed to her, but they kept either refusing or ignoring her request. We don't know what happened after that, but the pictures vanished.

—~~~—

We're just a few weeks from the due date. The doctor is seeing us weekly now. His new office is outside the city, in a district I've never been to, where millionaire mansions overlook whole stretches of sidewalks lined with cardboard shacks. Between the traffic and the confusing street network, we have a really hard time getting there. I'm so huge, so drowsy, so irritable, that I can't drive, and Alejandro—who hasn't often been behind the wheel in this city—finds it all particularly difficult. He says it's like the high level of a videogame (and that he has never been any good at videogames).

The gynecologist is now sharing office space with a Jewish doctor, whose children are usually playing in the reception area. There's no fish tank in the waiting room, but the secretary hasn't changed. The doctor can't do an ultrasound or weigh me because they haven't finished transferring his equipment. He gives me a superficial checkup and finds no change. He says there's no way he can tell if the baby will be born that day or a few weeks later. I inquire about one or two things that are bothering me; they are all "normal." In the blink of an eye, I'm outside his office and starting the interminable journey home.

I speak to Laura, who's in the same fix: the same doctor and the same problem of choosing a new hospital. She could go into labor at any moment. We visit the two suggested hospitals together and decide on the cheap one, which is closer to home. They assure us that the general facilities weren't damaged in the earthquake, although they are a little timeworn, and the maternity wards are new and in perfect condition.

I finally get Rachel's jokes about pregnancy on *Friends*.

I'm having lunch with Fátima in a restaurant that's not very good but is nearby. Although they say you have to walk as much as possible, it's so complicated; my range is limited and I quickly get short of breath. Fátima talks about how much she wants to have a child and the shortage of candidates to take on paternal responsibilities. She's come up with a plan. She can have a child with her mom, who wants to be a grandmother. Next year, Fátima will get pregnant (with the help of some male friend, perhaps, that's the easy part) and she and her mother can bring up the baby together. Brilliant, I say, it's a fantastic plan.

—⁓—

I'm past forty weeks but, inexplicably, the last few days have been easier. I suddenly feel better. If things continue like this, I don't mind waiting. I guess it's the calm before the storm.

—⁓—

I watch a short documentary in which Isabella Rossellini plays the role of *Diaea ergandros* (crab spider), the most self-sacrificing mother in the animal kingdom. When her children are born, she turns her body to mush so they can feed on her until she is totally consumed. Isabella Rossellini's spider says that this is the essential nature of all mothers and then, after a pause, adds: "Isn't it?"

I've always felt that my arms are longer than normal. That night I dream they turn into spider's legs.

—⁓—

I frequently saw my mother in the nude. She was never embarrassed: she'd shower in front of me, go into the sea naked when there was no one else on the beach; when she had her period she even changed her sanitary pad in my presence.

My grandmother was more prudish, but during the last years of her illness, when her incontinence pad had to be changed and she had to be helped to wash and dress, I also saw her naked on many occasions. I remember her yellowing skin with its prominent blue veins, her large breasts and very pale nipples, her curved back, her tiny toenails.

Close to her navel, my grandmother had a mole that both my mother and I have inherited. A satellite now in orbit on one side of my linea nigra.

———

In addition to the many depictions of her face, my mother painted one full-length self-portrait when she was pregnant. She gave it to my aunt, who had it framed and hung it in her home. One day, when she was dusting the painting, it fell into a bucket of water and dissolved.

III
white nights

Soon after midnight, two days after the due date, I got out of bed to go to the bathroom and felt as if a bucketful of water were running between my legs. On the phone, the doula told me that the contractions might begin at any moment; she said I should call the doctor and try to get some sleep, it could be quite a while before the time came to go to the hospital. I attempted to follow her advice, but the contractions started and the pain was very strong. I stood in the shower so the heat of the water would help me relax and then went back to bed. In the morning, my mother and aunt came by. With the help of Alejandro, they got me dressed and fed me bread and peanut butter. The pain was awful, but not as bad as I'd imagined, not as bad as the cramps I used to get as a teenager, which had me fainting every time my period came. At least there were gaps, moments of peace. At about 10 a.m. we spoke to the doctor on the phone and he told us to go to the hospital for an examination. I remember arriving, getting out of the car, and hugging my aunt as a contraction came on. A wheelchair. A light-filled, white room. Sitting in a white chair, waiting for the doctor to arrive. Unbearable pain when the gynecologist inserted two fingers into my vagina, and then relief when he said my cervix was dilated to nine centimeters. According to what I'd learned during the course and from books, the worst was over—all I had to do was push the baby out. After that everything is blurry. I got into a tub of warm water. Alejandro stood behind, hugging and stroking me. I was so tired that I fell asleep between contractions. They asked if I wanted to push; I didn't, but I tried. It was like walking in the dark and hurt like hell. When the doctor made digital vaginal examinations, I thought I was going to die. There were a lot of people there: Alejandro, the doctor, his assistant, the doula, my mother, the pediatrician, and a couple of nurses. Apart from Alejandro, who was almost as overwhelmed and exhausted as I was, everyone else was offering opinions. He held my hand tightly and I squeezed his; we were determined to go through the experience together. Maybe I should try getting down on all fours or sifting with a shawl they said. Maybe my blood pressure was low and it would be better to get out of the tub, maybe try a Maya chair. I had the impression of tension among the people in the room.

Antipathy. My mother had sneaked in without permission. I wanted her there but didn't have the energy to tell them. The doula gave me some water. It was cool. She said something kind, affectionate. The playlist we'd made in the previous days was coming through the speakers. The pain was unending. I remember telling Alejandro between contractions that I couldn't go on, that I was going to die. They say that you forget the pain of childbirth, and I have already forgotten it, but I retain a perfectly clear memory of those words related to that pain, words I otherwise had only ever used as a metaphor or hyperbole. The doctor listened to the baby's heartbeat every so often and we held our breath until we knew that it was fine. He didn't say anything, and that meant there was no problem. Then I remember being in a chair or some kind of folding bed. The doctor was speaking in short, unfinished sentences that sounded like he didn't understand what was going on, why the baby wasn't descending. I went on pushing, but I didn't know how to do it properly. In an irritable tone, he told me not to push that way, to push in a different direction. Then he said we were nearly there, that he could get the baby out with forceps. I refused the forceps, but he said he had another instrument, a kind of plunger. He asked if he could use it, and I said yes, whatever. And he used it. I felt myself tearing. Caetano Veloso was singing "O Leãozinho," the song Alejandro had played most frequently on the guitar during the pregnancy. I'd never experienced such pain, such fear, and such exhaustion. And neither had I experienced such relief, in every sense of that word, so much lightness, weightlessness, as when he was put to my breast and we looked at each other in silence. In the meantime, I was sewn up and the placenta emerged, but it was as if all that were happening to someone else; I was completely engrossed in him. His eyes were an absolute black, the whites scarcely visible. They were damp black eyes, like liquid obsidian, like live obsidian.

That first night in the hospital, before I could fall asleep, the nurse informed us that we should be on the alert because newborn babies sometimes forget to breathe. Naturally, we were terrified and didn't sleep a wink.

My aunts, mother, and cousin are in the living room watching him sleep in his tiny hammock while we chat. When he stirs or makes a sound, the conversation ceases and we all stop breathing for a moment.

My childbirth is over, but I have to imagine it. My childbirth or my son's? Whose is it? The person born or the one giving birth? Our childbirth. I experienced it but I didn't see it, so it's like a myth for me, something I have to imagine. Alejandro did see it and he tells me how the head appeared, surrounded by my pubic hair, and how, when the head was completely out, the doctor made him support the upper half of the body so that he could finish off the process. "Like those dads putting their children into the car seat," he says. The only person in my field of vision was the doctor. I had to ask, "Is he out?" And I watched him being laid on my breast. I want to witness a birth too, and I think if I'm born again, I want to be a midwife.

———

Adrienne Rich says: "No one mentions the psychic crisis of bearing a first child, the excitation of long-buried feelings about one's own mother, the sense of confused power and powerlessness, of being taken over on the one hand and of touching new physical and psychic potentialities on the other, a heightened sensibility which can be exhilarating, bewildering, and exhausting."

From the neck down, my body is a disaster area: tears, stitches, seeping blood. It's as if I'd exploded.

Sometimes I can't believe that he's been inside me. Where? How did a child of that size fit in there? I try to imagine him in the womb with the facial expressions and movements I can now see. It's almost impossible.

———

Virginia Woolf was advised against having children by her husband, her sister, and her doctor; they thought that motherhood would put too great a strain on her fragile mental health. On December 21, 1925, she notes in her diary that her friend and lover Vita Sackville-West, despite being "a little cold and off-hand with her boys," was "a real woman," something it is presumed Virginia cannot be since she has no experience of motherhood. Very near the end of her novel *Orlando*, there's an extremely strange scene full of hyperbolic euphemisms, so enigmatic that only in the last few sentences does it become clear that Orlando (the woman who was once a man) had been pregnant and has just given birth. Woolf, as no one before her, is mocking the taboos surrounding those two events.

In a photograph in *Vogue*, Woolf appears wearing a gown belonging to her mother, her sad eyes lowered. Her mother died when she was very young.

———

This afternoon, Laura and her two-week-old son came by to meet Silvestre. I'm surprised by how similar it feels to have her baby in my arms, the softness of his hair, his smell, the instant love I have for him. He could be my own, I think. I'm aware of the differences too: how quietly he cries in comparison to Silvestre; the ease with which he accepts his pacifier, which doesn't seem to interest my child. The two boys don't take much notice of each other, hardly even turn their heads to look.

I haven't seen Laura for a while, but we're in constant contact. Her tiredness and the pain from her C-section aren't noticeable, she looks as strong and cheerful as ever. Like almost all our visitors, the first thing she does is to ask me about the birth. I tell her what I remember clearly, which isn't much because in my mind the events are punctuated by a series of blank screens, which I attribute to the large amount of time I spent with my eyes closed. But as I talk, I begin to recall other scenes, I find words from some unknown source.

Laura listens, and when I've finished she tells me something about her own experience, something she hadn't wanted to mention before in case it made me fearful or prejudiced. Her labor was very long and ended in a caesarean due to a series of odd complications. That much I knew. What I wasn't aware of was that our doctor had displayed very little compassion, to the point of being almost aggressive. He'd frightened her, chided her for not immediately telling him when her water broke, and complained to his assistant about how long the birth was taking; he said he might have to cancel a breakfast appointment.

I hadn't found him particularly empathetic or kind during the birth either. I suddenly recalled his crossfit-trainer's voice telling me what to do, saying "not like that," almost angrily. I remembered feeling guilty, afraid, certain that something was going wrong. And then Laura and I were both furious; for each other.

This thing called "baby blues": I have bouts of crying when weariness and joy are mingled with a love so great it's almost agonizing. We take the baby for his newborn metabolic screening test. They take six drops of blood from his heel and I cry more than he does.

In English there's no sense of departure or splitting; mothers *give* birth. Margaret Atwood wonders: "But who gives it? And to whom is it given?" She definitely doesn't feel that it is "a gentle handing over" with "no coercion."

Time passes slowly at night and quickly during the day. I remember that poem by Seamus Heaney about St. Kevin, who stretched out his arms to pray, but his cell was so small he had to put one hand out the window, and a blackbird laid a clutch of eggs in his palm. St. Kevin waited for weeks with his arm stretched out until the chicks hatched and flew away. That's what pregnancy is like, what nights of breastfeeding are like.

My mother detested the gynecologist and thought the pediatrician was even worse. She was furious about the ice-cold way she treated the newly born Silvestre, as if she were manipulating an object, packing a bag, rather than putting the very first clothes on a living being who had just fallen to earth. So, while the pediatrician was measuring, weighing, and dressing him, my mother talked to Silvestre, whispered loving words in his ear.

A few days after Silvestre's birth I joined a breastfeeding chatroom. Two hundred or more women sharing tips on how to freeze milk, photographs of chafing on breasts, angry outbursts about unhelpful husbands, recommendations on brands of baby shoes, and hundreds of other things. I love and hate it at the same time.

For the last couple of days I've been keeping a close eye on the posts in the chatroom, feeling deeply worried. A child has cancer. His mother asks us to pray for him. I don't know how to pray and don't think it would do any good if I did, but I want to do something to help save that unknown child. He's on my mind all the time, I think of the photos his mother sends us. Maybe this is due to the hormones, but I don't believe it's normal to feel such anguish.

Next week I have to send in a report for the grant: a draft of the first pages of the book. I still can't recall what the point of the project was. With the computer on my lap, I open a file containing the notes I made, but workers are mixing concrete at a construction site nearby and the noise wakes Silvestre, who starts wailing.

Freud says that mothers can perceive the baby that was part of their own body as "an extraneous object."

In the mornings, lying in his crib, Silvestre fixes his eyes on the narrow strip of light entering between the drawn curtains as if he's trying to understand it.

Those involuntary smiles felt really strange at first. But it was even weirder to discover that I too smile very often during the day, without realizing it and for no apparent reason.

Once, during a trip to London with my mother, I left my wallet in the National Gallery. The following day we went back to retrieve it. It was pouring rain. As we came out, we saw some security guards dressed in yellow, sheltering by one of the oval windows in the façade. They smiled at us. My mother took a photograph and then painted an almost life-size image of it. It was one of her favorite works. During the earthquake it was broken in two.

Silvestre is in a good mood; he's laughing with his mouth wide open. I'd like to stay and play, but I leave him in Alejandro's care and take a shower. The shower has always been my place for thinking, for writing before I write, and now I'm trying to use my time efficiently. I attempt to think, but then I realize that I'm humming the cradlesong I sang to put Silvestre to sleep; it's about three bears getting ready for winter. I feel silly standing there under the water, singing a little song about bears, and then I hear him crying in the distance. I turn off the shower.

—⁓—

Louise Bourgeois's *The Birth* is a drypoint etching in red: the legs are open and the child is emerging like a diver with its arms stretched above its head. The ink seeps over the outline. Red fluid, like the water breaking and the blood pouring out.

—⁓—

Silvestre has been restless during the night. The milk in both my breasts has dried up, but he's still hungry and I spend quite a while transferring him from one breast to the other until the milk returns and he falls asleep. I lay him down, switch off the light, and get into bed, trying to make as little noise as possible. I think that I ought to write about the interruptions, the impossibility of writing. I should make a note of it. I should get my phone and make notes about all that, but the phone is very near Silvestre's head and I might disturb him, wake him. And, in any case, I'm beat and finally decide to sleep.

―⁓―

I don't know of any songs about childbirth and nursing a baby. There are one or two about pregnancy: Madonna's "Papa Don't Preach" and "Chica embarazada" by Gloria Trevi. What my friend said about pregnancy being a hangover, Gloria Trevi had already sung.

―⁓―

Breastfeeding is an act of faith. We don't see the milk the way we would water in a glass. We, the mothers, see the residue on the mouth of our children; we sometimes watch them devour it, but we never know how much they are drinking. In a brilliant essay, Margarita García Robayo says that breasts should be transparent.

―⁓―

It's three in the morning. I'm sitting up in bed, cushions behind my back and a feeding pillow across my thighs. Silvestre's head rests on my right forearm as he eats or drinks—I never know which verb to use for breastfeeding, because at this stage food and drink are the same thing. He's asleep but still feeding, making sounds that are sometimes like short sighs. As I have no other children and haven't been around many other babies, I used to think that they all make the same sounds, but Laura's child doesn't do this when he's sleeping. My nipples are less painful now. They only hurt a little when he latches. Each of the feeds lasts forty minutes so I try to find things to entertain me during that time; I don't want to fall asleep in this position (as has happened occasionally) and wake up two hours later with a crick in my neck. In my right hand, I hold my cellphone and scroll. I find an image, a drawing my friend Rachel made: a nude woman with two streams of milk springing from her breasts directly at the snouts of a pair of Xoloitzcuintle dogs. That image strongly reminds me of a sculpture in Parque México, the fountain I always refer to as "la chichona" due to her huge boobs. The statue is of a nude female figure with braided hair; she's standing upright, holding a pitcher under each arm. I discover that the sculptor was a man named Urbina, who was working in the thirties. The model was Luz Jiménez, and she turns out to be a fascinating person: an indigenous Nahua woman who posed for countless painters and photographers in the mid-twentieth century. There are portraits of her by Orozco, Rivera, and Leal, plus photographs by Edward Weston and Tina Modotti. I pause on a photograph by Modotti with the title *Baby Nursing (Conchita with Her Mother, Luz Jiménez)*.

———

Luz Jiménez: the woman with long braids, large breasts, strong arms, and wide shoulders. I'd seen her a thousand times without knowing who she was, or even realizing that it was the same model each time. I'd seen her as a water goddess in the Cárcamo de Dolores in Parque Chapultepec, as La Malinche in Orozco's *La familia*, and as that woman with tears in her eyes in Weston's photographs.

Julia Jiménez González was born in Milpa Alta, south of Mexico City, in 1897. She grew up speaking Nahuatl, learned to weave on a backstrap loom and to flip tortillas with her campesino parents; in the town's rural school, she learned Spanish. And that was her life until the Zapatistas came onto the scene. Julia remembered Zapata's arrival in the town, how he won the hearts and trust of everyone because he spoke Nahuatl. But after the magnificent Zapatistas came the Federal troops, who looted and raped, killed her uncle and her father. Julia and her mother fled to Xochimilco. They used to travel to the city to sell flowers and vegetables, and it was on one of those trips that Julia enrolled as a model at the Escuela de Pintura al Aire Libre of the Academia San Carlos. There's no clear evidence how she ended up there. A number of sources say that when she won a "spring maiden" beauty pageant, some of the painters invited her to model for them. Others claim that during her walks around the city she saw a flyer saying, "woman wanted for easy work," with the address of the academy. She began to pose wearing her everyday clothes and with her hair in its usual braids. And, as she had a charismatic personality and spoke Spanish, she became friendly with such artists as Diego Rivera, Fernando Leal, Jean Charlot, and David Alfaro Siqueiros. She showed them around her hometown and introduced them to the indigenous world there, so close to the city, yet so remote and seemingly unaltered by the Spanish conquest. It was at that time that she adopted the name by which her friends would know her from then on: Luz Jiménez. She was a model, but that didn't bring in enough to live on, so she also worked as a cook, tour guide, spinner, and domestic employee in the home of Frida and Diego, among others. The artists helped her. They were very fond of her. Rivera used to send a car to drive her from Milpa Alta, and she was treated as a member of the family; Charlot was a godparent to her daughter and the two corresponded throughout their lives.

The painters also introduced her to intellectuals; she soon also became a Nahuatl translator, teacher, and a source of information for the linguist Benjamin Lee Whorf. The journalist Anita Brenner published a book of the traditional Nahua stories that Luz told her, and there still exists a recording in which she narrates in Nahuatl the tale of a woman who goes to the river, is pecked by a bird, and as a result, becomes pregnant.

Luz herself was only pregnant once, and the father wasn't a bird but a sanitation inspector, who was very soon unfaithful, leaving her as a single mother even before her daughter Conchita's birth in 1925. They posed together for a number of painters and before Tina Modotti's lens. The years passed, and even though her youthful beauty transformed into the sober beauty of old age, artists still sought her out. There are many portraits in which her gray braids contrast with her brown skin. Luz was by then a legendary figure, the model who posed for the artistic greats. But money was still scarce. When Conchita's first child was born, Luz herself acted as midwife. Of the later portraits made of her, only a few of Tina Modotti's photos remain. She was run over by a truck and killed during a sitting.

I read that when a baby is breastfeeding, the vacuum effect causes the nipple to absorb a little of its saliva. The mother's body analyzes the saliva, detects any infection, and is capable of changing the composition of the milk, flooding it with antibodies.

Words are overrated.

———

Today I forgot to have breakfast.

———

Susan Griffin writes about the interruptions involved in motherhood and the fragmentation these produce. She says that we have only "brief illuminations" between the interruptions; interruptions that have to be recorded "side by side, hoping to make sense of it all some day later."

———

I've had a fever for three days due to an excess of milk. Silvestre is taking less than I produce, the ducts get blocked, and the result is a high temperature. Half delirious, I think: Milk is an action rather than a substance. Suction is needed to generate it; if the infant doesn't latch on to the breast, there's no milk. Milk is a bond. It's like electricity or magnetism: a form of energy that runs between two people when they are close. I read that even women who adopt children can produce milk when there is constant suction on the nipple. Milk is something that can happen when a child and a mother choose each other.

—•••—

A few days ago my aunt Maricarmen visited to meet Silvestre and, out of the blue, she reminded us that, when she was a child, an uncle of hers used to live in our apartment. "I was locked in that bathroom," she said, pointing to the door, "so I wouldn't see Rodrigo after the accident."

Since Silvestre was born, Rodrigo's ghost has been appearing to me. He died over fifty years ago, but goes on dying for all of us: his father, mother, and other women in the family, both those who knew him and those who didn't. I know the story by heart from so many retellings. His father (my great-uncle) and mother were away on a trip to Europe, their first journey since the births of their two sons—Rodrigo, age five, and Jorge, who was two. The boys were left in the care of my great-grandmother and my grandmother, who lived next door. One day the children went out for a walk with their nanny and everyone inside the house heard a crash. My great-grandmother, grandmother, and aunt Maricarmen, who was the same age as Jorge, came outside. A drunk had driven onto the sidewalk and hit the children. The youngest's injuries were awful but my grandmother, who in addition to being a doula was also a nurse, quickly realized that Rodrigo was bleeding internally. Someone had shut Maricarmen in the bathroom of the apartment we now inhabit so she wouldn't witness what was happening and then the others raced to the hospital. The oldest child died almost immediately and his brother was in very serious condition; he barely managed to survive spinal surgery.

The story goes that my great-grandmother never forgave herself for being incapable of protecting the children. Until the day she died, she would cry each time she recalled the incident. During my grandmother's final years, when dementia made her constantly anxious, the boy's ghost used to appear to her. She would ask about him: Where's the child? Who's looking after him?

My mother never knew Rodrigo, but she inherited the certainty that the whole world—including sidewalks, even the street corner outside her own home—is dangerous. Now that Silvestre exists, that same fear has taken ahold of me, my great-grandmother's fear, my grandmother's and my mother's fear. I too live on the corner where the accident occurred and every so often that child's face appears with the gap-toothed smile, ruffled hair, and almond-shaped eyes of the portrait my grandmother kept in a wooden trunk she called a *petaquilla*.

Rodrigo's mother used to say that she'd have committed suicide if it hadn't been for the younger child. I keep thinking of that incident because I believe it's a way of reducing the risk of it happening again. But sometimes it seems to me that when I imagine the events, I'm invoking them, and then I make an enormous effort to think of something else.

—⁓—

Silvestre is lying on my legs, I raise and lower my knees so that the rocking motion will amuse him. Two friends have come to discuss a recently published novel. I'm curious, say I'd like to read it too. Not yet, they reply. They don't explain why, but I can imagine a whole pile of reasons, mainly dead children. As if they know just how hard I try not to think about that subject these days. But still, I do. Since Silvestre's birth, I'm more fearful than ever. I know he's strong but he's tiny and looks so fragile. I find threats and dangers wherever I look. You should watch Truffaut's *Small Change*, my mother says; children are much more resilient than they seem. As if I had time for movies.

—⁓—

I spend the day mentally repeating the idea of writing about interruptions so that I don't forget it before I find a moment to write.

—⁓—

The photograph Tina Modotti took of Luz Jiménez frames her body from the shoulders to the hips, with a child of about one suckling at her large breast, visible beneath her shawl. Her white, loose-fitting blouse is pulled up to free the breast. The child's eyes are closed. Her hair is very short, black, and straight. She has a hooped earring in her lobe and is wearing a white dress with embroidery at the cuffs and neck. "The craftsmanship of the earring tells us that the child is an indigenous female," says an art critic. A shawl is draped over the woman's arms and below it the hands are crossed. The woman cradles the baby. We can't see her face, the people in the photo are not its subject; rather, it seems to be illustrating an abstraction: the act of breastfeeding. There is a continuum from pregnancy to weaning, a series of transformations in the body of the woman the purpose of which is, you could say, to *give* life. Even after the birth, when life has already been given, as she's nursing the child, the woman goes on giving life from her own life—from her time, her arms, her breasts, and her strength—to someone else. There's a long, long list of adjectives that can be used to describe breastfeeding: painful, delicious, exhausting, invigorating, awful, strange, and marvelous. Tina Modotti captures all that in her photograph. That state of being nourishment.

There's another photo, very similar but not exactly the same. It's a close-up: the blouse and arms are no longer visible, only the breast and the child's head; this time the eyes are half open, as if she's about to fall asleep, in that trance babies enter when they are feeding. This time the child's tiny hand rests on the breast. It's a very common gesture in babies, caressing the breast as they drink, playing. The morning after that nocturnal research, that is all I can remember: the child's hand. I must have fallen asleep not long after seeing it.

———

The cure for mastitis is to apply cold cabbage leaves to the breasts. The structure of the leaves is similar to the breast's. There's a poem in that, says Laura. I tell her that I don't write poetry and I don't believe in the cure.

———

Alejandro and I are translating a collection of short essays by Rivka Galchen; it's called *Little Labors* and is about babies. The book echoes our own experiences so closely that it seems more like Rivka is translating us, Alejandro says.

One of the fragments is almost identical to what

I wrote about *Frankenstein*. It compares the creature with a baby and Dr. Frankenstein with its mother. Plus it mentions the children that Mary Shelley lost and notes that her mother died in childbirth. Weeks later, I'm watching an Australian series, a comedy about motherhood, and there's the reference to Frankenstein again. It's impossible to be original when you write about being a mother. There are so many of us and our experiences have so much in common; despite any differences, we have so very much in common.

—␣␣—

Those first days must be terrible, says a cousin; after being so close for so long, your child goes to school. Yes, they are, my mother agrees. But it doesn't last. After a while you begin to feel amazingly happy to be alone.

—␣␣—

Adrienne Rich draws a comparison between nursing a child and sex. Breastfeeding, she says, "may be tense, physically painful, charged with cultural feelings of inadequacy and guilt; or like a sexual act it can be a physically delicious, elementally soothing experience, filled with a tender sensuality."

There is a painting by Monica Sjöö that shows a naked woman with her face half black and half white. In the background is an exterior space with planets, suns, and galaxies. The woman is giving birth; the baby's head is already outside her. Between her spread legs is an inscription that says *God Giving Birth*.

When the artist showed this work in 1970, the mayor of the English town of St Ives, where she lived, threatened to charge her with blasphemy and obscenity. He ordered her paintings to be removed, not just from the gallery but from the whole town. In that suffocating climate of intimidation, Sjöö was breastfeeding her second child.

My mother's painting *Emergencia* was practically unharmed in the earthquake. In obsessive, almost hyper-realistic detail, it depicts a shard of glass.

I have an app that notes which side I've nursed on and for how long. On average, it's a total of eight hours a day. That's a full working shift.

Writing while he sleeps. Reading while he feeds. Reading slim books I can hold in one hand. Writing from notes made on my phone while he's in my arms.

—◆◆◆—

Every time Silvestre cries I feel guilty: no matter the reason for his tears. We decided to bring him into the world and it seems to me that his happiness is our responsibility, whatever being happy might mean. He didn't ask to be born: we asked him. It's up to us, at least in the beginning, to make living worth the effort. To make it better than nothingness. "I had a child because life is better than nothing," says Marie Darrieussecq in *The Baby*.

—◆◆◆—

As a child I was always the first to hit the sack at sleepovers. I was afraid of staying up late because if I didn't get enough rest, I invariably woke with a headache. So many years of sleeping well and now I'm in a permanent state of insomnia. In the early hours, I was reading a book by Alice Munro on my phone. I loved it but am so tired that I hardly remember anything about it this morning.

My grandmother stopped assisting childbirths

because she hated the interrupted nights. She liked going to bed early and getting up before first light. She'd be on her feet at five in the morning and between the sheets by nine at night. But births generally happen at night and the hours of lost sleep wore her out.

—⁓—

During these first days of life, says D. W. Winnicott, the baby's activity consists of gathering "material for dreams."

—⁓—

I have an open book in my right hand. In the left I hold a breast pump to my right boob. One foot rocks Silvestre's rocker whenever it seems like he's ready to wake up. I've completely reconfigured the concept of multitasking.

—⁓—

During the whole of my childhood my mother was an abstract artist. When asked what she painted, I was enormously proud to be able to reply "abstracts."

—⁓—

In *The Millstone*, Margaret Drabble wrote: "It seemed

so absurd, to have this small living extension of myself."

———

I'm not sure what to think about the cult of milk. A book on lactation describes the breast as the perfect receptacle: hermetic but with uninterrupted transmission, the purest way to drink something straight from the source. There are a few women in the breastfeeding chatroom who think any problem can be solved with milk. One of the baby's eyes is red? Put in a few drops of milk. Her nose is blocked? A little milk in each nostril.

I've been trying to write for two hours. My mother has come to look after Silvestre for a while. She'll only call me if he's hungry. I'm transcribing these notes when she appears in the doorway saying that it must be reflux. Silvestre spat up a little milk while he was sleeping, and that means reflux is the cause of his grouchiness. She tells me to continue working but I've forgotten what I was doing.

———

There are days when I'm profoundly jealous of women who feed their babies formula.

———

A few years ago my mother and aunt came to visit me

in New York. One morning, we took the train to Dia Beacon: beautiful, frozen scenery along the Hudson Valley. We were in the Richter room with its huge, monochrome, reflective paintings, almost the same blue-gray as the frozen Hudson River. The three of us sat on a bench to view them and my mother took a photo of our reflection in the painting. Months later, she decided to paint that photograph, to reproduce that misty, phantasmal reflection. It was the first time she painted my portrait. We had video calls so that she could study the expression in my eyes, because it hadn't come across in the photo, she hadn't managed to capture it. The sensation was weird, like watching someone look through you, like being transparent. That canvas, which my mother painted after the collector's death, survived because it was accepted for the voluntary "Payment in Kind" scheme in lieu of taxes.

Apparently the oxytocin released during breastfeeding causes the mammalian brain to amplify the sounds of crying. Babies' cries trigger an instantaneous reaction in the most primitive areas of the brain. This oxytocin release can even result in postnatal depression and psychosis.

I've started wearing earplugs during the couple of hours Alejandro looks after Silvestre in the morning

so I'll sleep better, because if I hear anything even re-
motely like crying, including the cries of another child
outside on the street, I get anxious and wake. Even
so, I can't rest properly because I now dream that he's
crying to be fed but I can't find him.

I go back to the gynecologist so he can check the
stitches I needed after tearing during the birth. My
mother comes with me to take care of Silvestre. It's a
forty-five-minute drive each way along busy streets.
Silvestre is beside himself, crying; he needs movement
to keep him amused or lull him into sleep. I've resolved
to change doctors, find one whom I don't actively hate
and whose offices are closer to home, but it seems log-
ical that he should be the one to check his own work.
My mother and Silvestre stay in the waiting area. I
enter the examination room with some inexplicable
sense of fear. A few nights before I'd dreamed that my
vagina was being stitched closed. The nurse asks me
to strip from the waist down, except for my socks, and
then sit in the exam chair. The doctor will be here in
a moment, she says. On the door is a poster with photographs showing the correct postures for breastfeeding. As I attempt to concentrate on them a shiver runs
down my spine; I try to breathe deeply, to relax. The
doctor comes in and puts on a pair of surgical gloves;

they make a squeaking noise as he tugs them into position. Is it going to hurt? I ask, not completely sure what I'm referring to. He says I'm going to feel something cold and then a slight pinch. Since the labor, I've had a hard time imagining that anything could ever be more painful, but despite the strength gained from that experience, I'm still scared. It's all looking fine, he says. Everything as it should be. I can get dressed and he'll wait for me in the other room. He asks if I've had any discomfort. I mention one or two incidents of pain and he's unsurprised. If you experience bleeding like a faucet being turned on, call me, he says. Otherwise you're fine. And then he asks, with apparent curiosity—as if some other doctor had attended to me—how long my labor had been. I reply that my water broke at one in the morning and the baby was born at six that evening. But that's not the answer he's after, he says we all misunderstand that question. When did you arrive in the hospital? At eleven in the morning. And he was born at six? Yes. It was a long one, then. Very long, I repeat. And after a moment's silence he tells me he's moving to Playa del Carmen. He's been offered a job at a new clinic where he'll have interns and be able to live near the beach. Are your daughters staying here? Yes, they're staying, he responds. Why are you leaving? The argument with the other hospital had pissed him off. He wants to make a fresh start, have a new life. He's leaving next week but will come back once a month for consultations if I want to see him the following year. It's almost pleasurable to lie to him, say that I'm sure I will.

—⁓—

The grant committee refuses my request to modify the project. The change of topic is too drastic, the new project—this book—is very different. "But it will do you good to think of other things for a while, take your mind off the baby," says my advisor.

I give in. To complete the original project, I'll have to reread PhD theses, check official documents, and go to exhibitions. There are so many difficulties involved in leaving the apartment (plus: Silvestre doesn't like being in the car; he wants to feed all the time, and many places have no facilities for breastfeeding or what they have are inadequate; it's hard to manage him and the stroller at the same time, etc.), I have so little time for writing; maybe it would be better to write fiction. There's no other option. Using photos and old notes, I imagine myself in exhibition spaces, as if I had all the time in the world to stroll around them and, moreover, could do so on my own. My child is converting me into something I never intended to be: a novelist.

—⁓—

After giving birth, my mother, aunt, and their respective babies lived with my grandmother for a year. She looked after them, helped them during the interminable nights. My aunt says that she used to feel less worried when grandmother was with her son than when she was looking after him. I have the sensation that I gave birth to this child for them: my mother, my aunts, my grandmother. Like an offering. I had him for them and because of them; thanks to the unconditional love, security, and sense of community they offer, I was brave enough to have a child.

—

The other photographs in the series that Tina Modotti took of Luz and Conchita in 1927 tell a story. The camera frames them in close-up, showing their heads and just a little of the torsos. In one, the mother is explaining something they are both looking at. Their eyes are lowered, focused on the same spot, but the object of their gazes isn't visible, we only see Luz's parted lips as she speaks. In another photo, the mother is still talking while the child observes an object she holds in her small hand, something round and flat, maybe a coin. Perhaps the mother is explaining what a coin is. Perhaps she's asking the child not to put it in her mouth. In a third photo, the serious little girl looks into the eye of the camera, into the eyes of Tina, who is possibly talking to her. Luz, on the other hand, is looking elsewhere, as if her mind is on other things.

—∿—

I lost all sense of shame during the birth. So many people saw my body in its most vulnerable state, in its most grotesque and scatological transformation. Nothing related to its excretions or organs, none of the things it does feel embarrassing any longer. I only feel uncomfortable breastfeeding in public when I know it bothers the people around me.

"To hell with the baby," says the comedian Ali Wong during a stand-up show, "women have to stop working after the birth not to look after the baby, but to heal, to cure their broken bodies."

—∿—

When he's hungry, he's more like an animal. He opens his mouth wide and moves his head in a reptilian way, like a miniature dragon.

—∿—

My mother stopped painting from my birth to my second birthday in order to concentrate on raising me. "I didn't even pick up a pencil," she told me. Now she says that she was perhaps exaggerating, but I believe that, deep down, she expects me to do just that.

———

Silvestre sometimes falls asleep on my chest. He drops off while still feeding but can't bear to be put in his crib, or even in our bed. When that happens I lie on my back with him on my chest. I can feel his heartbeat, and I imagine he's once again inside me, his heart beating there.

———

Ten years ago, Mexico City's Museo Casa Estudio Diego Rivera y Frida Kahlo organized an exhibition about Luz Jiménez—the only one so far. Today I return to the museum accompanied by my mother, in search of a copy of the catalog. It's the first time I've taken Silvestre out for such a long stretch. It's still winter, the air is cold, but the sun is warm. Alfredo, the man who made a digital copy of the exhibition catalog, comes out onto the patio and asks us to wait on a sunny bench while he fetches the copy. Silvestre is hungry and grows restless. I unbutton my blouse and hold him close as he feeds. Alfredo returns with a CD containing the catalog and offers to give us a tour of the premises; Diego's studio, with his enormous papier-mâché figures, and Frida's small rooms. But Silvestre is still feeding so I tell them to go ahead and I'll join them when he's finished. Then Silvestre falls asleep and I'm unwilling to wake him. As time passes and the sun moves across the sky, I shift gradually to my left so he will feel the warmth but not have the light shining directly on his face. There's no backrest to the bench and my spine begins to ache. Silvestre wakes and I attempt to join the tour, but when we get to the external staircase that seems to float in the air—the trademark of the architect Juan O'Gorman— he begins to cry and I have to say a hurried farewell.

———

There are many theories about the moment a baby realizes that its body and its mother's are separate entities. I wonder at what moment a mother stops feeling that her child's body is also hers. The baby is outside of you but it came from inside you and is made of you, so it's still a little bit you. To what extent? Until when?

———

There's a quake in the night. The seismic alarm goes off. I grab Silvestre and the three of us run outside. The tremor wasn't strong but we're still startled. We wait in the street; it's cold, a neighbor takes off her jacket and wraps it around Silvestre. People assure us it's over. I return the jacket to its owner and we go back to the apartment. Silvestre slept through the whole thing.

—⁂—

Margaret Atwood wrote a short story in which she narrates a birth as if it were a horror story, with a level of suspense that makes one believe that something terrible is going to occur. What does happen is the birth of an enormous baby, a "boulder," which unhinges the woman's bones like "a birdcage turning slowly inside out." The narrator is writing the woman's story while her own daughter is taking a nap.

—⁂—

I want to write about Silvestre and the books. I have fifteen minutes to do it in, because my mother arrived to look after him but he immediately wanted to feed, then I needed to piss, and now my mother has to leave. I'm going to try to write quickly. Silvestre is nearly three months old. Apparently by that age babies can see and hear much more, and so now Silvestre is interested in everything. When he's feeding, he'll suddenly unlatch from the nipple and stare at the lamp or the wall, and what distracts him most are the bookshelves.

He's capable of spending minutes (that's a lot of attention for someone so young) looking at the books, and I wonder what he sees, if for him they are a single entity, like long worms or accordions. He's also beginning to hold things and for the first time is playing with a cloth book that makes a noise like a candy wrapper. He takes it in his hands, squeezes, shakes, and puts it in his mouth. I really like this totally visual, tactile, material relationship he has with books. I want to be able to see them as he does, if only for an instant.

In an attempt to reduce his extreme dislike of being in the car, we play Silvestre nursery songs. The only CD that distracts him, the only one he really enjoys, has traditional Mexican songs performed by children with shrill, jarring voices.

We're returning from an appointment with the pediatrician and the traffic is heavy. We listen to the whole CD, and when we get home Alejandro asks why all Mexican children's songs are about dead people. Rosario Castellanos wrote an essay about that. She says Mexican children treat death like a playmate. They are sung nursery songs about death and are lulled to sleep by fear, by the desire to escape. In the end death becomes so familiar that it's easy for them to laugh at it.

Some years ago, I read Valeria Luiselli's *Faces in the Crowd*, and I have never forgotten that fragment about how novels need "a sustained breath." The narrator has two children and they don't let her breathe. Everything she writes has to be in "short bursts." She's "short of breath."

Only one of the paintings completely disappeared in the earthquake: it was a portrait in which my mother is handing over another painting to her collector. She painted it in the medieval style of honoring the patron, with an inscription thanking him. Either my mother or I—not sure which—said that the collector had carried it off to the underworld with him.

Silvestre wakes every hour during the night. Alejandro is going to take him away in a few minutes so I can get a little uninterrupted sleep. I switch on the light and see him smiling, holding his feet, making excited sounds. It's his best time of day.

Alejandro tells me about the "little angel vigils" that are held in some parts of Chile when a newborn infant dies. They are called that because the baby goes directly to heaven; if anyone cries for the child, its journey will be harder. In "Rin del angelito," Violeta Parra sings about those children: "When the flesh dies, the soul searches on high for the meaning of a life cut short so early." Violeta wrote the song before her own daughter Rosa Clara died at the age of nine months. But she also wrote a song for Rosa Clara: "Verso por la niña muerta," a poem for the dead child. I almost didn't write this fragment from pure grief. When I hear those lines, those songs of sadness, it nearly kills me. Her grief and sorrow will be inscribed in the annals of history.

Several times a day I think about weaning Silvestre. Lately, my nipples have been hurting again, I'm not sure why. And I'm exhausted. My grandmother weaned my mother at three months and my mother weaned me at eight months. Nowadays, doctors advise breastfeeding for a year or, if possible, even two. I'm not sure I'll manage that.

Alejandro told me about a novel in which everything happens while a man is bottle-feeding his son. If I wean Silvestre, we won't love each other any less,

I think. We'll find other ways to show it. My grandmother and my mother; my mother and I: we found other ways to love each other. It's stupid to criticize women who decide not to breastfeed, whatever the reason. I don't even judge that character in Alice Munro's novel, the woman who smokes while breastfeeding her baby so she feels less like an animal.

———

This fragment in Daniela Rea's diary is so beautiful: "You slept through the whole night. My milk-full breasts spilled on the sheet. The stain looks like an old map." And I'm so damn jealous of that bit about sleeping through the night.

———

My mother goes to see the doctor, accompanied by her boyfriend and my aunt. She's had a pain in her side for months and can hardly walk now. They are gone for longer than expected.

In the meanwhile, Alejandro, Silvestre, and I have lunch with a Colombian friend and her children. Alondra has been living with a gay friend and his partner for six years. She got pregnant with one of them—doesn't know or care which—and had twins. The five of them now live in New York and she's visiting Mexico with the children.

My aunt calls and, without any further explanation, asks me to join them immediately. I leave everything: my friend, Silvestre, Alejandro, and the three large pizzas we've just ordered.

The tests have detected a two-centimeter tumor in her ovary. My mother is crying: quietly, she's not inconsolable. I hold back my tears and say we should see an oncologist right away. While they are making an appointment, I go to fetch Alejandro and Silvestre. I'm really sorry to have to say goodbye to my friend this way, so hurriedly, so clearly agitated.

IV
the tree of our flesh

Babies need happy parents; that's what they said in a documentary about child development. It's just been explained to me that my mother has to be admitted to the hospital, and I'm playing with Silvestre, thinking about how babies need happy parents.

—⁓—

I dream of the early morning when I was born. It's less a dream than a vision in a drowsy state of absolute weariness. I have the sensation that the darkness of our bedroom is the darkness of the womb, and that I'm small, minute, and the bed is a pair of hands holding me when I arrive in another, different kind of darkness.

—⁓—

My favorite fragment of Rivka Galchen's *Little Labors* states that "it's true what they say about a baby giving you a reason to live. But also, a baby is a reason that it is not permissible to die. There are days when this does not feel good."

There are whole days when the song about *La Llorona*, the weeping woman, sticks with me like an earworm. The legend goes that she's a mother who lost, or maybe even killed, her children; some say she's La Malinche, walking the streets, her face bathed in tears, calling out, "My poor children!" But in my mind, the song is in fact about a baby. A child who cries all the time. One of the reasons I think this is because of these lines: "If I have given you life, Llorona / What more do you want? Do you want more?" They can be read as both giving life and offering one's own life. I think about La Llorona a lot, particularly about this other variant of the lyric: "I love you more than life itself, Llorona / What more do you want? Do you want more?"

Tina Modotti was thirty-one when she took the photograph of Luz Jiménez breastfeeding Conchita. She had grown up in Italy and worked in a textile factory before her whole family migrated to the United States, where she became a model and actress. She'd arrived in Mexico five years before the photograph was taken, following her husband Roubaix de l'Abrie Richey. But Robo, as he was known, died almost as soon as he set foot on Mexican soil, and Tina left the country, only to later return with the photographer Edward Weston, who had been her lover in Los Angeles. Together they had decided to escape to the boiling pot of post-revolutionary Mexico.

The portraits that Weston took of Tina, as is also true of her self-portraits, clearly show the beauty that gave her a reputation as a femme fatale. Tina became Weston's student, but very soon distanced herself from his sublime aesthetic parameters, moving toward a documentary style of photography. It was then that she photographed Luz Jiménez nursing Conchita; a year or so afterward she gave up that art to concentrate on the political struggle.

Due to a uterine condition, Tina was unable to experience motherhood. There's no way of knowing whether her images of mothers and children, her gaze, are rooted in yearning or relief, but there is definitely curiosity there. In 1929 she took a picture of a pregnant Mexican woman carrying her naked child in one arm, and in 1930 took a very similar one of a pregnant German woman, also carrying a child. In both of these, as in the image of Luz Jiménez, the mothers' faces are not visible, and only in the final one can the child's face be seen. What interests her is the body language, the physical contact, the strength, ease, and assurance, the tenderness and the weariness in the physical bond between mother—double motherhood due to the pregnancy—and child.

—◆◆◆—

We meet at Laura's. The children are still not interacting much, although they do observe each other now for a few long, curious seconds. Laura tells me that her son is finally sleeping through for six hours a night. I'm green with envy. We laugh to see that the two boys have the same obsession with sucking their hands. She tells me hers can hold a bottle, and that now she can even go to her tango class one evening a week.

Someone has told Laura the real reason why our gynecologist went to Playa del Carmen. He'd delivered the child of a friend of a friend of hers, and the baby died. The doctor hadn't done the appropriate check at the right time and so they weren't aware that the umbilical cord was knotted around the baby's neck. My nails dug into the palms of my hands. Don't they say that's not really a problem, that the cord just unknots during birth? I ask Laura, because the teachers in the birthing class had been adamant that the whole thing was a myth to encourage mothers to opt for C-sections. Laura had thought so too. Maybe the rumor isn't true, or maybe the baby died of something else, she says. But it seems that the baby's death coincided with the doctor's departure from the hospital, a couple of weeks before Laura gave birth, three weeks before Silvestre was born. That whole affair of the sudden change of offices, the move to Playa del Carmen, sounds as if he's running away from something. I'm both furious and frightened. I tell Laura that even though our children are here, safe and sound, I'm scared. I'm fearing something that didn't happen, fearing a possibility.

We're silent. I'm thinking over the birth, the lack of ultrasound scans in the final stages of my pregnancy. It could have been my child. I imagine death sitting silently among the doctors and nurses in the maternity unit. Nearby, as close as life. A playmate. I fear Silvestre's suffering in every verbal tense and mood: the present, the future, the past, even the conditional perfect; he might have suffered.

—⁓—

"If I die, everything's in order. It wouldn't be too big a deal. The only reason I refuse to die is so my daughter won't suffer," says my mother in the hospital.

—⁓—

Ten years after Tina Modotti took the photo of Luz Jiménez, Frida Kahlo, who was a friend of Tina's, painted *My Nurse and I*. A large, brown-skinned woman, her features covered by a black mask, is breastfeeding the child Frida, who has an adult face. Milk dribbles from both breasts and in one of them the glands show through the skin like a sprig of white flowers. Rain, as pale as milk, is falling from the sky onto the green foliage, and also onto a whitish leaf, a rain of milky sap.

Frida was born only eleven months after her sister Cristina. As her mother was unable to breastfeed her, she had an indigenous wet nurse. In an interview, Frida said that this was the origin of the painting. She herself never breastfed; all her pregnancies ended in miscarriages, which was one of her greatest sorrows.

The woman in the painting has no face because she represents an abstraction: the indigenous Mexican culture that nourished Frida all her life.

Instead of a face, she has a mask, which represents Coatlicue, the mother goddess, the goddess of the earth who suckled the stars that shine in the sky like that rain of milk.

She has no face, in the same way life and death have no face.

Babies are born without tears. During their first months, they cry without tears. Maybe this is because they cry so much and it would be impractical to be constantly bathed in salt water. That the crying is dry causes me much greater anguish.

The Mexica people believed that babies who did not survive the first months of life went to a paradise where there was a "suckling tree" with leaves from which milk flowed. The sixteenth century Florentine Codex explains it this way: "It is said that when little children die, like jade, turquoises, and jewels, they do not go to the cold, fearful region of the dead (Mictlán). They go to the house of Tonacatecuhtli; they live beside the tree of our flesh. They suck the flowers of our sustenance: they live beside the tree of our flesh, they are suckling beside it." The tree of our flesh. The tree of our flesh.

A while before getting pregnant I became a vegetarian. It wasn't a premeditated decision. After reading about the environmental tragedies that result from the global market for red meat—something I'd never been keen on regardless—I decided to avoid eating it.

Then the idea of ingesting it began to revolt me and one day, several months later, I realized that I was a vegetarian. I'd never dream of expressing any moral superiority over carnivores; it was a personal decision. But I have to admit to liking the idea that, during my pregnancy, the material forming Silvestre's body didn't derive from animal carcasses. There was something symbolic but also superstitious in the notion that at least his first months of his life had no connection to that form of death and violence.

The truth is that it wasn't really hard for me to only eat vegetables and grains because, during the whole time I lived with her, my mother never cooked meat. I ate it in other places, at my grandparents' and friends' homes, but there was never any meat in our house.

The day the oncologist gave us the news of my mother's tumor, the first thing my indignant aunt said was, "But why? She's a vegetarian."

My mother refuses to let Silvestre visit the hospital. In addition to all the germs floating around in the air, her refusal has to do with the ambience of the place. Children shouldn't be in hospitals, she insists. Babies need happy parents. I have to leave her regularly to feed Silvestre at a nearby restaurant where Alejandro is entertaining him.

The digital catalog that Alfredo gave me has a number of essays about Luz Jiménez and a compendium of the paintings and photographs in which she features. It also has a video about her life that finishes with a series of images; many of them are in the compendium but there are also other, very different ones. For example, a black-and-white photograph that makes me pause the video. It's a shot of three female figures: a nude Luz Jiménez with her keen-eyed gaze, a braid draped over one shoulder; another, older woman, gazing into space in the right-hand corner, whom I take to be Luz's mother; and in the center of the image, in Luz's arms, is a tiny newborn baby with black hair. The contrast of black and white, the tints and reflections, give the image a ghostly aura, as if it were a composition involving three specters. It must be a childbirth image, I tell myself, because of Luz's nakedness and the tiny infant. The unreality, the otherworldliness of that scene is like childbirth, which opens a portal between the underworld and this earth, between death and life.

There's no credit for that image in the video. I'm unable to contact Luz Jiménez's grandson, who might be able to identify it; when I ask Alfredo and the art historians I know, none of them have any idea how to get in touch with him or can attribute the photograph.

Who is Luz looking at so intensely? Not the child's father, who had disappeared off the map by then. So, for whom were those three females posing? Who was the witness? Could it have been Tina behind the camera?

—*—

During the first year of her child's life, says Alice Walker, everything she wrote sounded "as though a baby were screaming right through the middle of it."

—*—

It may be the endorphins released during breastfeeding that have been making me feel so upbeat lately. Even when I'm decidedly sad or angry, a part of me is deliciously, ridiculously happy. There are moments like that, when I'm completely split in two.

—*—

I've changed my mind. My favorite fragment of *Little Labors* is the section "Sometimes It Can Seem Like Many Hours with a Baby." It goes like this: "If you discovered you could communicate with a chimpanzee, would you give that up? Or would you spend near on all your hours with the other species?"

I Google the gynecologist to see if any complaints have been posted about him. Instead, I find his Twitter account. It's more or less up to date, has around twenty followers, and is divided into three main areas: Buddhism, photos of his daughters, and photos of the deliveries he's overseen. There are hashtags everywhere: #loveisreal; #loveandcompassion; #dontbeafraidofchange; #grandesoportunidadestodoslosdias; #lovetoday. I show Alejandro the feed and he immediately scrolls to the date of Silvestre's birth. Under a Tweet that says "the pain of living old dogs," and under #partorespetado, #Parto Humanizado, and #loveand-compassion, there is a five-second video in which Silvestre appears, naked on a towel, his hair damp and his eyes half shut. I believe that he's lying on my chest and in the last second my hand appears, moving toward him. He has a slight grimace on his face. Beneath the video is a blurry photo, but I know it shows Alejandro and I hugging during the birth.

I'm furious. I have no words to express the violence of someone taking those photographs and that video without our permission, and then using them for self-promotion. That he would decide to make a record of that supremely vulnerable moment of our lives without our consent. That, at a time when I was feeling the world had both come to an end but was also beginning, the doctor was focused on making a video with his phone to post to his Twitter account. My head practically exploded with rage.

―――

I try to set myself one task each day. Just one: cut my nails or send an email. But I don't manage it. There's no time.

I write here: *There's no time*, and I think those words are true in two senses: when you have a baby, there's very little time, and when you have a baby time is annulled.

―――

Of the paintings that survived the earthquake intact, the first to appear from the rubble was one of my favorites: my grandmother's hands. It's a small, square, life-size portrayal of her long, strong, bony, wrinkled hands painted in black and white, one resting on the other.

―――

One of the minor characters in *The Book of Lamentations* is an indigenous woman who's forced to act as the wet nurse for the daughter of some landowners. They take her son away so that she'll only breastfeed their daughter, and the indigenous child dies. During the remainder of the novel, she loves and cares for the girl as if she were her own. This heartrending tale is told in just a few lines.

—⁓—

We have another family story, related to my great-grandmother's sisters. They lived in one of those colonial houses without hallways so that to use the bathroom, you had to pass through everyone else's bedrooms. Cruz, one of the sisters, married very young and her husband, a general, went to fight in Mexico's Cristero War. When he returned, years later, he lived in the family home. One night, the general got the younger sister, Marta, pregnant: he mixed up the rooms and either seduced or raped her; no one knows which. Marta was sent away to spend her pregnancy in Acapulco and the twins she bore were given up for adoption. She never married. Cruz stayed with the general until he died some years later. She never had children. Although both sisters were writers, they never wrote about any of that.

—⁓—

The tumor is in the right ovary. My mother says it makes biological sense for her ovaries to give up the ghost, because they are no longer any use; they have fulfilled their purpose and two generations now carry her genes. If it were just a matter of age, I tell her, or of reproductive function, there would be no children with cancer. She finds that argument convincing.

―――――

The Mexicas thought of childbirth as a pitched battle. Women who died while giving birth became either a *mochihuaquetze*, a courageous woman, or a *cihuateteo*, a divine woman. Warriors coveted the fingers and hair from the corpses of these women, because they were believed to give them strength in battle. It was thought that when women died in this way they accompanied the sun on its journey. They lived in the western part of the sky, in the region of evening, which was known as "The place of women."

―――――

There's no end to fear now, Tania tells me. It starts in the first months of pregnancy, with the fear of miscarriage and the birth, of childhood illnesses; it changes form, but stays with you for the rest of your life. I've just watched a documentary that explains that this is not only a psychological reaction, but also biological: a part of the mother's brain—or that of any person who is a primary caregiver—directly related to fear is switched on during child rearing and remains that way through the rest of the parent's life. There's no way to turn it off.

For Sheila Heti, the part of motherhood that frightens her most is its endlessness, "its eternity."

—*w*—

Ten years before Tina took the photograph of Luz Jiménez, another immigrant who would end her days in Mexico made a print called *Maternidad*, motherhood. Angelina Beloff was born in Russia and had studied painting and printmaking in Saint Petersburg and Paris. When she met Diego Rivera in Belgium, they fell in love and got married in 1911; in 1916, she had a son, Diego, who died of cold and starvation at the age of fourteen months. Following that catastrophe she produced *Maternidad*, possibly based on a photo or her own memories. The artist is seated on a wooden chair. She's wearing a thin, short-sleeved blouse, which makes me think that it must be summer in France—one of those white nights when darkness falls only briefly. One breast is uncovered and she holds an infant in her arms. Angelina is looking down at the nursing child, who is almost asleep, his eyes closed. Behind the chair, a cat observes the scene with its proverbial curiosity.

The image contains absolutely no trace of grief or any premonition of death. There is only the tranquility of the moment, the particular sense of peace of a child finally drowsing at the breast after constant movement, laughter, restlessness, and crying.

After the child's death, Diego Rivera painted a portrait of Angelina breastfeeding, which is also called *Motherhood,* although with the addition of "*Angelina and the Child Diego.*" But this one is a cubist portrait and gives the impression of being an experiment in form and color.

—*⁓*—

My grandmother was the eldest of seven children. But she often altered the story when I asked about it. She wasn't the eldest, another girl had been born before her but had died very soon afterward. There were eight children, not seven—her mother had eight pregnancies, had given birth eight times. It was important to remember that.

I read that after a pregnancy, even one that doesn't reach full term, the fetal cells go on floating in the mother's uterus. They continue to be part of her body for up to forty years. I read this just a few days before my mother's womb is removed.

In all those births she assisted, had my grandmother seen a baby die? A mother?

Silvestre is sleeping. It's eight in the evening. I should take advantage of these moments to sleep too but can't, and I'm too tired to work or read. I browse Facebook. I browse Laura's Facebook page in search of any of her friends or acquaintances who seem to have been pregnant. I'm following up on that rumor of the child who died in the gynecologist's care. After a few minutes, I come across a graphic designer who is pregnant in several photographs, all taken months before. Pregnant in China, pregnant in the metro, pregnant in a forest, pregnant with two other women hugging her. Then that's it. She hasn't uploaded any photographs since.

The woman has curly hair. She teaches typography and makes event invitations to order. In two or three photos she appears with a young child I guess is her daughter. If anything ever happened to Silvestre, I'd commit suicide. That's what I think whenever I consider the rumor. I'd be incapable of bearing it. The problem arises if you already have another child, like my aunt and uncle, like this woman on Facebook. You can't kill yourself, and that must be torture. Like being a zombie, a vampire, or a ghost; one of the living dead.

No, my aunt says, my grandmother never saw a mother or child die during the birth. There was just one baby who came very close to death. Just one, and he survived.

Mothers who write, according to Ursula K. Le Guin, are "almost a taboo topic." The reason is that they "have been told that they ought not to try to be both a mother and a writer because both the kids and the books will pay—because it can't be done—because it is unnatural."

A few days after giving birth, Nahua women undergo the temazcal purification ritual with their midwives. It takes place in a cave; the midwife heats stones, onto which she pours water to create steam. She also boils plants, salvia real, *hierba de ángel*, *tabardillo*, pineapple, and bay leaves. The mother lies on a woven mat and the midwife wafts the steam over her using bunches of leaves. They stay in the temazcal as long as the mother's body can tolerate the heat.

Luz Jiménez's grandson turned up and told me the story of the ghostly photograph. They are in a temazcal. The spectral quality of the image is due to the dark backdrop and the haze of water evaporating from the hot rocks. The photographer is unknown.

The paintings my mother did during my infancy all had to do with what she was reading. She did one series on the *Koran* and another on Goethe's *Faust*. She read various editions of the latter book in several languages and used to quote from it to the point of tedium. The series on *Faust* was one of my favorites back then because there were witches. That wasn't actually true, but I imagined them among the splashes of colors, in the sparks flying from the dark purples. One from that series was a canvas called *El lugar de las madres*, the realm of the mothers. It was cobalt green with a sort of heart in the center floating in primeval waters, surrounded by unicellular marine creatures.

When Faust asks Mephistopheles to help him bring Helen of Troy back to life, he replies that she can be found in the realm of the mothers, a place without time or space, in the absolute emptiness of the depths of the depths. The womb of the universe. The word "mothers" suddenly sounds strange to Faust, as if "mama" was not the first word most infants utter, the original, most familiar word in the world. Or maybe it's exactly for that reason, because it embodies the mystery of creation, that it seems strange to him.

Silvestre says *mamá* all the time these days, but it's

still like a burble, not really a word, and he only bur-
bles it when he's unhappy; when he's happy he makes
a whole load of other sounds.

—⁓—

My mother recalls this story:

My great-grandfather's sister, Lola, was married to a
man who was just a little more macho than was normal, even for that time. He wouldn't allow her to read,
in spite of the fact that it was her greatest pleasure in
life. Discounting breastfeeding. Each time her husband found out that the new baby was a girl he'd stop
talking to her for months, and she would take advantage of the situation to read. Lola had nine daughters,
breastfed all of them, and during those almost nine
years of nursing her offspring, she read a great deal
and read freely.

—⁓—

While Silvestre is sleeping I write this fragment based
on the notes I've made on my phone. I know I have
only a little time so I stick to the point. I write from
the sheer joy of being able to do so.

—⁓—

When she was pregnant with me, my mother used to enjoy imagining which member of the family I'd take after. If I'd have my father's eyebrows, my grandmother's nose, grandfather's eyes. She thought about it often, until one day when she looked in the mirror and, for the first time, the possibility occurred to her that I might resemble *her*. At first she was startled by the idea, but then she told herself that it wasn't so bad. It wouldn't be a major crisis if we looked alike, as long as I was born with straight hair.

Having curly hair has been the bane of her life. In the seventies, when she was growing up, it was unfashionable and she tried out hundreds of straightening techniques and treatments. Those wavy locks that always seemed so beautiful to me, were an annoyance for her; she even thought her curls were corny.

Like me, Silvestre has straight hair, although during the first days it was hard to tell since he had almost none. His hair started to grow at more or less the same time as mine began to fall out. During pregnancy there is less hair loss than usual, but from the fourth to the seventh months of nursing it falls out in handfuls. Now that my mother is also experiencing hair loss due to her chemotherapy, there are three of us in the same state: Silvestre, my mother, and I are all half bald. Alejandro decided to cut his own hair in solidarity and did it so badly that he can nearly be added to the tally.

One of Silvestre's favorite pastimes is pulling off his grandmother's turban. She makes faces at him and he laughs loudly.

―――

Silvestre has no long-term memory, and these days neither do I. More than ever before, I live in the present, focused on what he needs, wants, and does at any given moment. And that moment swells, the days are so long that I feel as if years rather than months have gone by since his birth. I live in a place without time, in the realm of the mothers.

―――

I suffered a muscular spasm in my lower back at the very worst moment: the morning after Alejandro had left for a ten-day trip to Chile. Now I can't move. So much carrying Silvestre and feeding him in awkward positions have taken their toll. I move into my mother's house; she can't help me because she's going through those really tough days after the chemo. The two of us are bedbound wrecks. But my mother's German boyfriend is staying with her; he's a darling and looks after Silvestre. He takes him for *Kliene Spaziergänge*, short walks around the house and garden, and then to the neighbors—my aunts, uncle, and a cousin—who alternate responsibility for Silvestre, show him Margarita's necklaces, Marisa's maracas, and Héctor's red wooden truck. My cousin, who is two meters tall, hoists him up onto his shoulders, and Silvestre delights in the panoramic view.

They return him to me when he's hungry, and between feeds I read. In this really amusing novel by Diego Vecchio, *La extinción de las especies*, the narrator tells us that in the Kiataw language there are many different ways of saying *mother*:

> *Ka'tsill*: the mother who gives birth to a female
> *Ka'tsoll*: the mother who gives birth to a male
> *Ka'tusbel*: the mother of daylight hours
> *Ka'twenak*: the mother of the night (a word that
>   can also mean ancient secret or ancient woman
>   who hides something)
> *Ka'takan*: the double mother (the mother who is
>   mother of a mother)
> *Ka'uchkan*: the mother who can no longer become
>   a mother—like mine

We start to fill one of our diaries with Silvestre's firsts. Beginning with his first solid meal, which we make into an avocado (for me, *aguacate*; for Alejandro, *palta*) ceremony. We laugh and clap so much that he looks at us like we've lost our minds. He seems to know perfectly well how to eat avocados, as if he's done it thousands of times before.

My aunt kept a diary for many years with curious anecdotes about my childhood. The entry for October 1991, when I was three, says: "We were in Tepoztlán and Jazmina was waiting for her mother. Suddenly she said that she wanted to be her own mother."

Another entry, this time from November 20 of the same year, says something similar: "Jazmina said to her mother: 'I wish I'd been born from myself.'"

—————

These are some of the things that have been said to my friends when they were breastfeeding in public:

"Cover yourself. Don't give the waiters the pleasure."
"Cover yourself. Don't be such an exhibitionist."
"Would you like me to help you cover yourself?"
"They won't even let you in here wearing shorts.
    What makes you think you can breastfeed?"
"Wow. Check that out."
"Ugh. What an awful sight."
"Aren't you embarrassed?"
"Only Indians breastfeed. Civilized people use
    formula."
"Would you like to use the restroom to do that?"

On the patio of my grandmother's house there used to be an ancient fig tree. When I was a child it was over a hundred years old. The figs were delicious, I'm told (I don't like figs so can't corroborate that), and it was full of birds throughout the whole year. The trunk had so many knots that it was easy to climb. My cousin and I used to pretend it was our horse.

During earthquakes, my grandmother would run out onto the patio, and—although she wasn't religious—would hug the fig tree and repeat in a terrified voice: "Christ, calm your wrath."

It seems wrong that trees also die, that they don't live forever. The fig tree finally succumbed to old age a few years ago.

My grandmother passed away in the same bed she was born in. Perhaps not exactly the same bed, but it was in the same house and in a bed that was very near to where the one she was born in had stood. She came into the world and died on the same soil and, like the fig tree, succumbed to old age.

In my mother's opinion, some paintings were improved by the intervention of an earthquake. Paintings she hadn't liked, but with the addition of cracks and other surface mishaps, she now does, or at least more than before.

—⁓—

I'm sorting my earring box, checking for single ones and deciding which I don't really care for and can give to people who would. I find a pair of studs in the form of a *calavera,* a skull, that I bought some years ago. I've always liked gothic imagery: skulls, bats, wolves. I have a crow tattoo on my right shoulder. I consider my calavera earrings and think that I should give them away. Babies need happy parents. Should I really be writing this book?

—⁓—

Western culture generally holds that women should have babies and not concern themselves with writing books. "That women should have books rather than babies is a variation on that theme," according to Alicia Ostriker.

—⁓—

I have to sit down and write the other book, the one for the grant. I *must* sit down and write that book, whereas this one writes itself. I write it but it writes itself, like Silvestre in my womb.

—⁓—

After giving birth, some women experience phantom kicking in their bellies. My mother says that she has phantom hair. She still feels the need to wash and brush it, despite being bald.

—⁓—

The self-portrait of Catherine Opie nursing: her full, nude torso on which the viewer can just make out the scars spelling out the word "Pervert," her short hair, the tattoos on her arm, her large breasts, her serious expression, her gaze fixed on the blond baby feeding at her right breast. In the background, a red and gold Victorian tapestry.

It is both a tribute to and a parody of a 1906 painting by Mary Cassatt: *Young Mother Nursing Her Child*. The same pose, the same gaze. The difference is that Cassatt's baby is holding its mother's chin. Well, in fact, that's one of hundreds of differences.

—⁓—

While I'm nursing Silvestre in one of the chairs in the bookstore my mother browses the table of new titles. In the children's area, a father is reading his daughter a book about Frida Kahlo. My mother passes near them to listen. The book is open to the painting of the wet nurse feeding Frida, and the little girl asks why she's wearing a mask. The father says it's because Frida was afraid of the wet nurse because she was a bad person. My mother moves on, looking at the books for a moment. When she returns the father and daughter are still on the same page. The temptation is too much. She tells them that it's not true. The wet nurse is wearing a mask because she represents the pre-Hispanic, indigenous world that Frida loved, and that nourished her throughout her whole life.

Slightly disconcerted, the father thanks her and my mother returns to us, having unburdened herself.

In a collection of essays on motherhood by Anna Prushinskaya, I find this extract: "To say that I am gaining independence is strange, as one can't quite become independent from another part of oneself." And further on, another beautiful idea: "We are all a history of someone else's limbs."

While Silvestre is playing with Alejandro, I write, but half my brain is still focused on my son. I pause when he cries; the impulse to be with them is almost as strong when I hear him laugh. Sometimes there's nothing to do: I get up and ask what they are laughing about.

—◦◦—

During the first months of breastfeeding, Silvestre took so long that we looked like we were sitting for a portrait the whole day: him feeding, me with a book. Now it's impossible to read. He kicks, as if he were dancing. Sometimes he unlatches for a moment, looks into my eyes and makes a sound, as though he wants to comment on something, then he reconnects to the nipple. We often have to isolate ourselves during his feeds, go to a place where there are no people because he's distracted by his surroundings. In the past, he never rejected the breast, but now he does just that quite frequently. Whenever the world interests him more than food.

—◦◦—

This book should finish with weaning. Begin with pregnancy and end with weaning. That was the plan: for the narrative thread to be the body, the transformations of the body. The plan for this book didn't include earthquakes or mothers with cancer.

Winnicott says that during the first months of a baby's life, time isn't measured by clocks or by sunrise and sunset, but by the maternal heartbeat, her respiration rate, the rises and falls in stress, and other non-mechanical devices. There is no time in the realm of the mothers.

Whenever I write something in the "first-times" notebook I'm filled with anxiety. Because every moment of his life feels like the first time for something: the first time he ate ice cream, the first time he waved at his reflection, the first time he made that gorgeous sound I should have taped. I'd like to be able to record everything, his whole life up to this moment. But my anxiety is due to the fact that almost all the firsts also involve lasts.

The first time he ate solids: the last time he was a milk-only baby.

I receive a visit from two friends who neither have nor want to have children, and who have no children in their family circles or among their close acquaintances. They sit at the dining table and I stay with them for a while, but Silvestre is doing his "momism" stuff. Separation anxiety, the manuals call it. It's a stage that occurs when babies begin to understand that they and their mothers are separate beings and that the latter will sometimes go away. It lasts until around the age of two. If I leave Silvestre, he sets off a shrill alarm. If we're in the same room, he demands that I stay close to him. So on this occasion Alejandro is unable to amuse him for long, and Silvestre ends up playing with me on the colored mat. He refuses to crawl, but can already walk if someone holds his hands, and that's what he wants to do all day long, be led from one place to another in the apartment. I attempt to talk to my guests, shouting in their general direction, but there are too many interruptions.

The women have their eyes fixed on their phones, only occasionally looking at me with a mix of revulsion, compassion, and boredom. And yet they don't go. From their elevated position at the table, they tell me to leave Silvestre and come with them to a bar where another friend is waiting for us. When I try to explain why I can't just get up and accompany them, they clearly think I'm exaggerating or just being a killjoy. For the first time, I'm pleased when Silvestre cries. I hope he'll cry louder. Scream. I'm dying for them to leave. Standing in the doorway, just before their departure, they ask me how I'm doing. I'm tired, I say, and close the door.

"Of course there's hardly anything written by women about pregnancy and breastfeeding. When are they supposed to write? And the little time you do have, you want to write about other things—about explorers, martial arts, anything else." That's what Gala says. She's a writer with a one-year-old. We're at home, chatting while our children sleep. At that moment, two memories come almost simultaneously into my mind. First, that advisor from the grant committee who said, "It will do you good to think of other things." And also a story by Shirley Jackson about a pregnant woman who is fed up with thinking about her pregnancy and only wants to read reports of murders in the newspaper.

They are sensible women. They are absolutely right to want to distract themselves, get outside their own heads. I want to do that too, but I don't know how; I can't think of anything else, and neither can I stop thinking, except when I'm writing. If I write everything that I think, I'll be able to stop thinking. That's what I believe. What I hope.

The first time my grandmother assisted during labor was when her sister gave birth. After that she helped dozens of women in our extended family, plus friends and acquaintances. She used to tell us of how surprised she was that sometimes quite reserved, neurotic women turned out to be very good at childbirth; while, for example, an Italian woman with wide hips whom she was certain would have absolutely no trouble had suffered a great deal, crying nonstop from the very beginning. She also used to tell us of a Japanese woman who, on each of the three occasions she went into labor, locked herself in the bathroom and refused to let anyone in. They had to break the lock to get her out.

She never charged for her classes or assistance, but the women used to give her jewelry, works of art, and bone china in thanks. She gained the lifelong affection of many of those women.

———

For Zadie Smith, being a mother was, initially, a form of displacement:

It forced me, at least partially, into a secondary position in my own life. Even the simple biological recognition that my daughter is on the way in and I am unavoidably on the way out. And time-wise, it made me very impatient of wasting any. Even my sentences have the stench of motherhood upon them. I haven't the time for elaborate metaphors! I want to get to the point—to be understood.

—∿—

In a bookstore café, I can feel Silvestre wriggling under the shawl as I try to feed him. After partial success, I leave the store and see a woman walking along the street, breastfeeding as she goes, the child in her arms and her boob in full view, as if it were the most natural thing in the world. She seems like a splendid Amazon. It occurs to me that, when it comes to nursing a child, the awkwardness is the problem of the person who feels it. I put the shawl in the diaper bag and when we get home Silvestre waves it about and wraps it around his wrists.

—∿—

The most difficult thing to write about is the happiness. There's not much to say about that simple, clear, almost ridiculous happiness I feel eighty times a day. Examples: when Alejandro plays the guitar and Silvestre listens; when he recognizes his grandmother and laughs; when I open the door and he squeals with delight because he knows we're going for a walk.

—∿—

In a self-portrait my mother painted a year or two ago, she's holding an empty frame up to a landscape. Her back is to the viewer, her hair is loose, and she's looking toward some mountains. That's how it must feel to be a painter; making your way through the world, your back turned to it, with a frame in your head, in your eyes. During the earthquake, a hole appeared in the canvas of that painting, close to the frame. A round hole, as if a bullet had passed through it.

———

In relation to childbirth, Maggie Nelson says: "If all goes well, the baby will make it out alive, and so will you. Nonetheless, you will have touched death along the way."

———

I've almost returned to my pre-pregnancy weight now. I'm looking like myself again. The black line is still there, but lighter. I don't want it to vanish. I read that this line exists on the bodies of almost all women before they become pregnant, but the color is very similar to their skin tone. During pregnancy, it darkens.

The vertical scar from my mother's surgery is in the same place and is almost the same length as the linea nigra.

My mother, her boyfriend Martin, Silvestre, and I go to the Museo de Arte Moderno to see the Leonora Carrington exhibition. It's the final Sunday and apparently thousands of other people have decided to do exactly the same. A security guard at the entrance asks us to check the stroller into the cloakroom. The woman in the cloakroom laughs—there's no space left, we'll have to take it with us. Still carrying the stroller, I go to the end of the long, long line, while my mother, Martin, and Silvestre play in the garden.

A uniformed woman approaches to inform me that I won't be able to enter the exhibition with an empty stroller. Pardon? I ask in confusion. If you have a baby, it has to be in the stroller, she says. I explain that I do have a baby, but he's not with me at this moment, and he'll become very restless if he has to sit in the stroller while we go through the exhibition; he'll cry and then I'll have to carry him. If he cries, says the woman, you'll probably have to go outside.

Martin offers to put the stroller in the car. Silvestre doesn't want to leave the garden; he has a new friend, a boy named Carlitos who is letting him play with his toy cars. We drag him unwillingly away. My mother has Silvestre in her arms. The line moves forward. We go into the first room.

Carrington herself had two children and the fey,

mythological universes she invented contain a number of mothers. Mother goddesses who care for tiny eggs and spectral infants.

My favorite piece is a wooden cradle with wheels and sails. It has real and imaginary animals painted on the sides, like a cosmic Noah's ark. The cradle was carved by José Horna and belonged to Norah Horna, daughter of the Hungarian photographer Kati Horna. In the final room of the exhibition there is a childhood photograph of Norah sitting in the cradle, laughing.

Silvestre observes the paintings carefully, and looks just as carefully at the other viewers. When he sees a horse, a unicorn, or a Pegasus, he clicks his tongue; when he sees a cat, he beckons it to come to him. The sight of a red mask makes him squeal with delight.

—

In a bookstore, during a group discussion about *Little Labors*, a man in the audience says that he doesn't understand why motherhood has suddenly become such a popular topic in literature. "It's not clear to me why anyone would be interested," he said.

I know of other female authors who are also writing about pregnancy, childbirth, and breastfeeding. More fragmented texts that quote from *The Pillow*

Book. I love this new mode of writing and hope that it will become much more than a fashion. That there will be more of us. Many more. In my opinion, there will never be enough of us. I think of newspapers, lists, letters, herbals, textbooks, pregnancy journals and diaries, homemade cookbooks: all these forms of writing are, or can be, literature. The same thing is true of baby diaries. I want there to be more than enough of them, and for them to be good, bad, or indifferent books. I want a canon and a tradition. And also a rupture, counter-canon books. New literary genres.

―――

Rineke Dijkstra made portraits of three of her friends: Julie, Tecla, and Saskia. The photographs were taken a few hours after each of them had given birth. The women stand naked in their homes in Holland (a country where the majority of women have home births). One of them is wearing an herbal postpartum sanitary pad, another has a visible caesarean scar, and the third has a trickle of blood on her calf. All of them are cradling their newborns to their breasts. One covers her infant's eyes to protect them from the flash. Dijkstra decided to take these photographs after accompanying a friend during her labor.

I keep fantasizing about becoming a doula. I imagine the courses I would have to take, the friends who would allow me to help them. Accompanying childbirths must be addictive. As if you were able to see the Big Bang more than once.

—ᴡᴡ—

Before restoring (or deciding not to restore) her works, my mother wants to show them in the half-ruined state they were left in after the September 19 earthquake. She wants the exhibition to be held on the anniversary of that event.

—ᴡᴡ—

Rachel Cusk: "I realise that a person now exists who is me, but who is not confined to my body."

—ᴡᴡ—

Jacqueline Rose: Motherhood "is a way of being inhabited by the other."

—ᴡᴡ—

After the death of my grandparents, after living for seven years with a grandmother suffering from advanced dementia, elderly people used to make me think of a poem by Patrick Kavanagh:

Every old man I see
Reminds me of my father
When he had fallen in love with death
One time when sheaves were gathered.
…
Every old man I see
In October-coloured weather
Seems to say to me
"I was once your father."

Every old woman I see reminds me of the long evenings attempting to amuse my grandmother, taking her out for walks, exercising patience when she became anxious, when she got angry and insulted us. Every old woman I see reminds me of the brief moments of lucidity when she recognized me, and the very few occasions when my mother managed to make her laugh.

Something similar now happens to me with children and babies. I'm really interested in them, and if I observe one for more than a minute, I invariably feel that I could love that child as if it were my own. That it could be my child, that I could make it my child.

———

One day it occurs to me just how many books, movies, songs, and tales there are about dying and death. Innumerable stories about death, yet so few about birth.

"It seems to me a pity that so many women, including myself, have accepted this denial of their own experience and narrowed their perception to fit it, writing as if their sexuality were limited to copulation, as if they knew nothing about pregnancy, birth, nursing, mothering, puberty, menstruation, menopause, except what men are willing to hear, nothing except what men are willing to hear about housework, childwork, lifework, war, peace, living, and dying as experienced in the female body and mind and imagination. Writing the body, as Woolf urged, is only the beginning. We have to rewrite the world.

"White writing, the French feminist Hélène Cixous calls it, writing in milk, in mother's milk. I like that image, because even among feminists, the woman writer has been more often considered in her sexuality as a lover than in her sexuality as pregnant-bearing-nursing-childcaring."

That lesson on writing from an article by Ursula K. Le Guin is the most important thing I've read in the last months. If it wasn't so long, I'd have it tattooed on my body.

The story on the digital catalog narrated by Luz Jiménez in Nahuatl is almost identical to the pre-Hispanic myth of Coatlicue.

Coatlicue was the mother goddess; the goddess of the earth who gave birth to the sun, humans, animals, and the stars. Once, when she was sweeping, a ball of fine feathers fell from the sky beside her. She picked it up and placed it on her breast. When she'd finished sweeping, she looked for the feathers but couldn't find them. At that moment she became pregnant with the sun god, Huitzilopochtli.

In Mexico City's Museo Nacional de Antropología there's a statue of Coatlicue, with her skirt of snakes and her death mask. Two breasts are carved in the stone of the torso; they sag from having suckled the whole cosmos.

~~~

The Polish artist Elka Krajewska founded the Salvage Art Institute (SAI) in which she brought together forty works by recognized artists that the insurers had declared to be damaged in transit, by fire, flood, or an act of vandalism. When a work can't be restored or the cost of restoration exceeds its value, the insurers pay the market price and dump the damaged piece in a basement. I found out about this institute in a novel by Ben Lerner and want to read that passage to my mother. She tells me to wait until after her next surgery. She'll be bedbound for three weeks, unable to paint. She says she'll read the book better then.

—⁓—

The earthquake and my ailing mother. The instability of what seemed most solid.

—⁓—

"Babies eat manuscripts," says Ursula K. Le Guin. "The poem not written because the baby cried, the novel put aside because of a pregnancy, and so on. Babies eat books. But they spit out wads of them that can be taped back together." Or maybe not. Maybe better to leave what the earthquake broke as it is.

—⁓—

We organize a first aid course for a number of friends who have babies. It's going to take place one afternoon at my mother's house because she has more space than we do. In the morning, Alejandro isn't feeling well; it's the start of one of those migraines that can knock him out for weeks, even months. We're terrified. No medication has ever been any use, but a friend who had the same problem suggested magic mushrooms. Alejandro gets ahold of some and stays home to try out the new treatment.

While he's doing that, in my mother's house we're attempting to memorize the steps of CPR and practice them on some revolting mannequins, to the accompanying wails of five babies under a year old. Then we try to copy down the list of potential hazards in the home.

Stairs; windows; knives; hot pans on the stove; electronic equipment that is plugged in at the wall; furniture not fixed to the floor that could topple onto an infant; cleaning fluids it might drink; pills it might swallow; heavy objects it could pull down onto its head; the pillows in its crib; buckets of water or the toilet bowl, where it could drown, because infants like putting their heads in water but then can't manage to pull that heavy weight back out.

I could rewrite Edward Gorey's alphabet of dead children with all this devastating information. I'm considering permanently relocating to a hospital room when Alejandro begins to send me text messages: "Tripin aint so difrent to flyin an im still lisnin to silvio rodriguez. An im arging wit the ants. I put ???? on my ???? Now I undustan, it mus be hard t crawl."

———

It seems to me awfully unfair to my mother that I don't remember anything of the first two years of my life. Biology is so unkind to mothers, not allowing their children to recall the times when we were closest to them. I'd like to invent those memories, the way

Anaïs Barbeau-Lavalette does. She says that she used to drink her mother's milk with the same intensity she now makes love, as if it were the last time.

—ᴡᴡ—

Another painting that survived the earthquake was based on a photo I took. My mother was working on a small canvas—Grandma's hands—on a table that's been in her studio for as long as I can remember. The table was splattered with multicolored blobs of paint, like a Pollock canvas. On it were the painting, a brush, and my mother's glasses. I took a picture of the arrangement and my mother painted it. Her painting in the painting. My photo in her painting. My grandma's hands, my mother's eyes, and me behind a camera, looking at them.

—ᴡᴡ—

I think about white nights and sleepless nights. About those nights in Russia and Alaska when the sun never sets. And that short story by Dostoyevsky of the same name about unrequited love. I think about the term "white nights": nights that are days, as white and sleepless as mine. As white as milk.

—ᴡᴡ—

Whales move around in schools and some species such as orcas have mother-only groups. Orca calves can't dive as deep as their mothers, so when they go hunting they leave their young in the care of other mothers, who sometimes even nurse them. The females nurse their calves for two years; their milk has a high fat content, is a sort of paste that can pass through seawater without dissipating.

In the center of the Biblioteca Vasconcelos in Mexico City, the skeleton of a whale, the work of Gabriel Orozco, is suspended in the air. It's the Sunday of World Breastfeeding Week. Under Orozco's whale, fifty of us are nursing our three-, six-, and nine-month-old babies; some wearing nursing bras, others not; some sitting, others standing; some with a partner, others alone or with a female friend. For a few minutes we are like whales: a community of lactating mothers immersed in a sea of books.

———

In the photograph, I'm wrapped in a pink shawl. My mother's flannel nightshirt (identical to the one I wear now) is unbuttoned. A ray of light enters through the window and falls on us. I'm about to start feeding or have just finished, separated from, but still very close to, my mother's breast. She's looking at me with an ambiguous smile, a Mona Lisa smile.

Terry Tempest Williams says that her mother's voice is a lullaby in her cells: "When I am still, my body feels her breathing."

—⁓—

Microchimerism refers to the exchange of fetal and maternal cells in the womb. The term comes from the Chimera of Greek myth, a monster made up of the parts of various animals. The fetus's cells are able to pass into the mother's body through the bloodstream, but the maternal cells can also enter the fetal body through the placenta. And, although this is less likely, a grandmother's cells may also enter her grandchild's body. As fetal cells are capable of adapting to the maternal tissue—like foreigners learning a new language—they insert themselves in various organs to become part of the mother's body. We are made of others. This is a microchimeric book.

—⁓—

Paula Modersohn-Becker painted several portraits of women breastfeeding, and although she only nursed for a short time (the twenty days before her death), she captured certain specific gestures that I have never before seen portrayed. For example, the way a mother takes her nipple between her fingers to offer it to the baby. Or the baby who becomes distracted because the artist attracts its attention when the mother wants it to feed. Or that painting, now one of my favorites, in which a naked woman lies, like some other mammal—a cat or a dog—with her equally naked baby lying next to her, feeding. In the book I'm reading about Modersohn-Becker, the author, Marie Darrieussecq, notes how comfortable this posture is, and how it is so rarely represented. Silvestre feeds that way almost every night.

———

From the themes, ideas, and anecdotes that my obsessive mother has been repeating for as long as I can remember, two things have become very clear to me:

1. Paintings can't be reproduced by photographic means. They have to be seen firsthand, close up, from a distance, calmly, because painting is not image; it is matter.

2. The etymological root of the word "matter" is the Latin *mater*: mother.

———

In the afternoons, my mother comes over to help me bathe Silvestre. He likes bath time; he puts on a surprised expression and plays with his feet, although he also grabs my sleeve, as if from an instinctive fear of drowning. My mother sings him a song about ducks. She lets him play in the water for a few minutes before taking him out and passing a comb through his scarce hair. Silvestre always wants to feed after his bath. We sit in the wicker chair and he drinks my milk until he falls asleep. Breastfeeding is less strange now; it's not so painful and feels more natural, more pleasant. Nevertheless, it's still often exhausting and exasperating. While Silvestre feeds, my mother sits on the edge of the bed and we chat. This afternoon, I tell her that a friend came to photograph Silvestre and it hadn't occurred to me to ask him to take a portrait of me nursing him. I need a photograph of that because at some point it's going to stop and I'll want to remember it. My mother takes out her cellphone. I never think of her as a photographer because she's a painter, but all her life she's taken shots with her camera or her phone, and many of her canvases are based on those images. She crouches and asks me to move my right hand because the perspective looks odd. A few minutes later, she sends me a series of six photos. Some are full-face, others taken from above. My blouse is open, a braid of hair lies on my right shoulder, and it seems as if my eyes are closed, but that's because I'm looking at Silvestre. He's lying on a cushion in his white pajamas and is clutching the fabric of my blouse. There's no way of telling from the photo, but I know that his eyes are indeed closed.

breastfeeding resources

I read almost all of these on my cellphone, although I was able to hold the lightest physical copies in one hand. Some I read all the way through, others just excerpts. I was reading many of them for the first time, others for the second or third. The list includes books, individual poems, short stories, interviews, and essays. Quite a few of them are quoted in this book and there are many others I'd have liked to quote. Not all of them have to do with motherhood, but I'm pretty certain that they were all written by someone born of a woman. I've listed them in the approximate order in which they were read.

Like a Mother by Angela Garbes
Roedores (Rodents) by Paula Bonet
Motherhood by Sheila Heti
Mamasutra (Mothersutra) by Paz Calderón Hoffmann
The Argonauts by Maggie Nelson

¿Cómo se hacen los niños? (How are babies made?) by Ana
    Westley

The Book of Lamentations by Rosario Castellanos, Tr. Esther
    Allen

Mothers: An Essay on Love and Cruelty by Jacqueline Rose

Are You My Mother? by Alison Bechdel

Women, Art, and Society by Whitney Chadwick

The Second Sex by Simone de Beauvoir, Tr. Constance Borde

Nine Moons by Gabriela Wiener, Tr. Jessica Powell

Of Woman Born: Motherhood as Experience and Institution by
    Adrienne Rich

"The Boatman" by Katie Schmid

Sin palabras (Without words) by Paloma Valdivia

The Sexual Night by Pascal Quignard, Tr. Chris Turner

Obras completas (Complete works) by Sor Juana Inés de la Cruz

Ensayos (Essays) by Natalia Ginzburg, Tr. Mercedes Corral

Mother Reader: Essential Writings on Motherhood, an anthology
    edited by Moyra Davey; particularly:

        "Giving Birth" by Margaret Atwood

        "The Old Dictionary" by Lydia Davis

        "The Fisherwoman's Daughter" by Ursula K. Le
            Guin

        "A Wild Surmise: Motherhood and Poetry" by
            Alicia Ostriker

        "A Writer Because of, Not in Spite of, Her Children"
            by Alice Walker

        "One Child of One's Own: A Meaningful Digression
            within the Work(s)" by Alice Walker

Novels and Stories by Shirley Jackson

Orlando: *A Biography* by Virginia Woolf

Poesía no eres tú (You are not poetry) by Rosario Castellanos

"White Nights" by Fyodor Dostoyevsky, Tr. Constance Garnett

Tarantela by Abril Castillo

Suzanne by Anaïs Barbeau-Lavalette, Tr. Rhonda Mullins

Diario de quedar embarazada (Pregnancy diary) by Claudia Apablaza

The Millstone by Margaret Drabble

"On Narcissism: An Introduction" by Sigmund Freud, Tr. James Strachey

Ina May's Guide to Childbirth by Ina May Gaskin

The Great Mother: Women, Maternity, and Power in Art and Visual Culture, 1900–2015, catalog for the exhibition curated by Massimiliano Gioni

Marlene Dumas by Dominic Van den Boogerd, et al.

Louise Bourgeois: I Have Been to Hell and Back, reprint by Iris Müller-Westermann, et al.

Faust by J. W. Goethe, Tr. David Luke

"The Lenny Interview: Zadie Smith" by Lena Dunham

Three Women by Sylvia Plath

Kahlo by Andrea Kettenmann

The Diary of Frida Kahlo: *An Intimate Self-Portrait* by Frida Kahlo and Sara M. Lowe

"St Kevin and the Blackbird" by Seamus Heaney

Little Labors by Rivka Galchen

The Luminous Novel by Mario Levrero, Tr. Annie McDermott

Germinal by Tania Tagle (unpublished)

Faces in the Crowd by Valeria Luiselli, Tr. Christina MacSweeney

The Baby by Marie Darrieussecq, Tr. Penny Hueston

The Long Goodbye: *A Memoir* by Meghan O'Rourke

Frankenstein by Mary Shelley

Ongoingness: *The End of a Diary/300 Arguments* by Sarah
   Manguso

La extinción de las especies (Species extinction) by Diego Vecchio

Natural Histories by Guadalupe Nettel, Tr. J. T. Lichtenstein

Being Here Is Everything: The Life of Paula Modersohn-Becker
   by Marie Darrieussecq, Tr. Penny Hueston

Dept. of Speculation by Jenny Offill

"Memory of My Father" by Patrick Kavanagh

A Woman Is a Woman Until She Is a Mother by Anna Prushinskaya

A Life's Work: *On Becoming a Mother* by Rachel Cusk

Primera persona (First person) by Margarita García Robayo

Lives of Mothers & Daughters: *Growing Up with Alice Munro* by
   Sheila Munro

El parto sin dolor (Painless childbirth) by Consuelo Ruiz
   Vélez-Frías

*Una mujer sin país: Las cartas a Edward Weston y otros papeles
   personales* (A stateless woman: Letters to Edward Weston
   and other personal documents), edited by Antonio Saborit

"Naciste en mí antes que en el mundo" (You were born in
   me before you were born into the world) by Sara
   Schulz

When Women Were Birds by Terry Tempest Williams

The Stud Book by Monica Drake

Babies and Their Mothers by D. W. Winnicott

"Mientras las niñas duermen" (While the girls are sleeping)
    by Daniela Rea

In Vitro by Isabel Zapata

JAZMINA BARRERA was born in Mexico City in 1988. A former fellow at the Foundation for Mexican Letters, she has a Master's Degree in Creative Writing in Spanish from New York University, which she completed with the support of a Fulbright grant. Her book of essays *Foreign Body/Cuerpo extraño* was awarded the Latin American Voices prize from Literal Publishing in 2013. In 2020, Two Lines Press published her *On Lighthouses* in translation from Christina MacSweeney. She has also published work in various print and digital media, such as *Nexos*, *Este País*, *Dossier*, *Vice*, *El Malpensante*, *Letras Libres*, and *Tierra Adentro*. A grantee of the Young Creators program at FONCA, she is editor and cofounder of Ediciones Antílope. She lives in Mexico City.

CHRISTINA MACSWEENEY received the 2016 Valle Inclán prize for her translation of Valeria Luiselli's *The Story of My Teeth*, and *Among Strange Victims* (Daniel Saldaña París) was a finalist for the 2017 Best Translated Book Award. Among the other authors she has translated are: Elvira Navarro (*A Working Woman*; *Rabbit Island*), Verónica Gerber Bicecci (*Empty Set*; *Palabras migrantes/Migrant Words*), and Julián Herbert (*Tomb Song*; *The House of the Pain of Others*).